EXPERIENCE BIBLICAL EVANGELISM WORKBOOK

PRACTICAL INSIGHT FOR DAILY EVANGELISM

MARGARET ADJOGA-OTU

EXPERIENCE BIBLICAL EVANGELISM WORKBOOK

Practical Insight For Daily Evangelism

Published by God's Life Publishing
5369 Edgewater Dr, Ewa Beach, HI 98706

Email: godlife@aol.com   www.godslifepublishing.org

This book or parts thereof may not be reproduced in any form, stored in a retrieval system, or transmitted in any form by any means—electronic, mechanical, photocopy, recording, or otherwise for commercial gain or profit—without prior written permission of the publisher. The use of short quotations or occasional page copying for personal or group study is permitted and encouraged.

Unless otherwise identified, Scripture quotations are from the King James Version of the Bible.

Cover design & layout
by God's Life Publishing

Copyright ©2019 by Margaret Adjoga-Otu
All rights reserved

International Standard Book Number: 978-1-950315-00-0
E-book ISBN: 978-1-950315-01-7
Printed in the United States of America

Dedication

I would like to dedicate this book to my Lord and Savior, Jesus Christ; who chose me to be his evangelist. I am humbled by this endeavor; moreover, I am extremely grateful for His mercy and grace in allowing me another chance to write this book although I was initially reluctant a year prior.

I want to thank the evangelist by the name of Steve who gave me my first gospel tract, that produced the fruit of my salvation. Also, my sincere thanks to God's Life Christian Church for supplying the gospel tracts to the evangelist.

I would like to thank my Pastor and father in the gospel, Bishop Calvin Bethea, for seeing my potential and repeatedly telling me over a decade ago that I should write a book on evangelism. My heartfelt thanks also goes to my Co-Pastor and mother in the gospel, Dr. Melrose Bethea, for encouraging me to go past my limits with this book when I thought I had nothing left. I also want to thank every prayer partner or every person I've ever prayed with concerning the lost. May the Lord perpetually keep the fire burning in us all!

A special thanks to every person who was willing to hear me share the gospel message and receive Jesus Christ as Lord and Savior.

TABLE OF CONTENTS

Preface	7
Introduction	9
Foreword	11
Chapter 1: WHAT IS EVANGELISM?	13
Chapter 2: THE GOAL OF EVANGELISM?	21
Chapter 3: YOUR DUTY TO EVANGELIZE	29
Chapter 4: THE ROLE OF THE EVANGELIST	35
Chapter 5: HINDRANCES TO WITNESSING	45
Chapter 6: FURTHERING THE GOSPEL	63
Chapter 7: CONSEQUENCES FOR NOT WITNESSING	73
Chapter 8: BENEFITS OF WITNESSING	77
Final Words/Conclusion	83
Answer Key	84
About the Author	85

PREFACE
EXPERIENCE BIBLICAL EVANGELISM WORKBOOK

How To Use This Workbook

Experience Biblical Evangelism has been written to dispel the misunderstanding about evangelism and to equip the believer with a practical tool to become a person of wisdom who wins souls. I encourage you to read all the scriptural references and complete every assignment to deepen your understanding of evangelism and to motivate you to plant and water the seeds for harvest. Practical and beneficial insights are provided for the new convert or the seasoned saint who wants to *Experience Biblical Evangelism*. Use this workbook, for reflection and spiritual growth, for group Bible study and Sunday School discussion. Groups using this workbook are encouraged to use the reflections as a springboard to facilitate, explore and discuss various aspect of evangelism. For your convenience an answer key is provided at the back of this workbook.

Each chapter in this workbook has a review section with the following elements:

Chapter Theme:
The main idea of each chapter is summarized for emphasis and clarity.

Questions for Reflection:
A few questions are given to bring about introspection and encourage conversation for small group study or discussion on the topic.

Exploring God's Principles:
Questions and review material are provided to highlight and summarize the teaching points that I have developed from the Scriptures and personal experience.

Applying God's Principles:
Additional questions and suggestion for prayer and personal action are provided to help the reader or group participant apply the study material to his/her life.

This section includes three parts:
- *Thinking It Over*
- *Praying About It*
- *Acting On God's Truth*

One of the most important things we can find out about ourselves and God is why God redeemed our lives from destruction with a command to "Go ye".

God's plan for evangelism will clearly unfold before you.

You will see evangelism as the ultimate pursuit and experience that will satisfy your thirsty soul and enlarge God's kingdom.

Introduction

I was reared in the church and went faithfully every Sunday. Though I was an usher, sang solos in the choir, participated in the Soup Kitchen Ministry, made a junior deaconess, and had given trial sermons at the age of 16; sadly, I had not even heard of the term "saved" or "born-again" at my church. I assumed that those two terms were church lingo designated for certain denominations. When God had sent different people to me asking if I were saved, I wasn't sure. I had never heard of it. I had to be saved, I thought! After all, I was a faithful churchgoer participating in all these "church" activities; I did all these works, and that had to serve as my VIP card into heaven, right?

One day, the Lord orchestrated my path and caused me to have an encounter with an evangelist like Phillip in the Book of Acts. He was an older heavyset Caucasian man who several times a week for years stood on a corner in downtown Newark, New Jersey passing out gospel tracts/booklets. Though this is an urban area heavily populated with black and brown students, he diligently positioned himself near a busy bus stop and offered to everyone these little booklets. It did not matter that he appeared to stand out like a sore thumb; he was mission-minded. My best friend and I took one from him one day and it was the beginning of my life being transformed. I saw the address, and promised myself that I would visit one day.

A series of events guided me to pray a similar prayer like the one in the back of those little booklets/tracts. As a result, I repented of my sins and received Christ in my heart. Months later, I was invited to a church service and it turned out to be the place that was stamped on the tract/booklet that I had previously received from the evangelist. Like the eunuch, I received a fuller understanding of Christ, was baptized with the Holy Ghost and currently is an evangelist and minister at that same church that was on the back of the Chick tract.

Upon receiving Christ as my Lord and Savior at 16 years old, I was relieved that I was finally positive of my salvation. Nevertheless, I grew increasingly concerned about the spiritual state of others, both in and out of the church. Right away, I counted it my duty
to warn people and beckon them to come to the Father through Jesus Christ. Understanding that time is running out, God has used me to lead many to salvation and discipleship because of these experiences.

Furthermore, this subject is near and dear to my heart because there are messages preached about soul-winning and its importance without giving practical guidance.

While evangelism and salvation experiences may vary from person to person, "Experience Biblical Evangelism" will answer the following questions:
-What is evangelism?

-Where do I begin?

-What should I do next?

-How do I acquire a burden for the lost?

As you read this book, I encourage you not to rush through its chapters. Rather, take your time and allow Holy Spirit to minister to you. May this workbook richly bless you in your witnessing endeavors.

Foreword

God has always had the Apostles, the Prophets, the **Evangelists,** Pastors and Teachers as His kingdom specialists. Their chief focus was to establish a Biblical foundation in which the work of the kingdom could be advanced to the extent of souls being saved and disciples being made.

One of the most misunderstood callings and title usages in the church is that of the Evangelist. The title of an Evangelist has been loosely given particularly to women in the church for numerous reasons other than as a testimony and confirmation that the individual was called and burdened by God to labor for souls to be saved. Many of those individuals do not demonstrate any of the characteristics of the actual work of the Evangelist. There is little physical evidence that they are passing out gospel tracts, witnessing to the lost, inviting unbelievers to seek a relationship with Christ, or fasting and praying for conviction and repentance in the unsaved.

As the senior and Founding Pastor of God's Life Christian Church, I conferred the title of Evangelist on Margaret Adjoga-Otu because she had demonstrated that she was a genuine and consist soul-winner. This observation was birthed in me, when she brought six people with her from her college to what was only her second Bible Study night at the church. From then on, it was evident that she had a hunger and burden for souls to be saved. She has consistently brought carloads of people to church over the years with the intent of introducing or watering the gospel in their lives. It is normal to observe her engaging strangers with the gospel wherever she finds herself. Her pursuit of obeying the Great Commission has led many to Christ and discipleship.

As a spiritual father to Evangelist Margaret Adjoga-Otu, who has served for two decades under my tutelage, it excites me to see what God has done through her efforts to evangelize. This book is from the heart and life of one who is truly called by God to the sacred office of Evangelist. She has a genuine commitment to win souls and see them become disciples. She shows this in her lifestyle as an Evangelist who is also a worship leader, Bible school teacher and capable minister of the gospel.

When people ask me for an excellent resource to accompany a study of Matthew 28:19-20 **(Evangelism)**. I will recommend this workbook and tell them that the author is a chosen vessel with a track record of seeking and winning the lost.

Bishop Calvin L. Bethea, *Senior and Founding Pastor*
God's Life Christian Church, *Irvington, New Jersey and Ewa Beach, Hawaii*

CHAPTER 1

WHAT IS EVANGELISM?

"To evangelize is so to present Jesus Christ in the power of the Holy Spirit, that men shall come to put their trust in God through Him, to accept Him as their Savior, and serve Him as their King in the fellowship of his church."

-William Temple-

What does it mean to witness or evangelize?

Before we look at what it is, it's quite important to understand what it is not.

Evangelism Is Not The Following:

1. It is not aggressively pinning a person against the wall, while demanding that he or she accept Christ as Lord and Savior. It is not a means by which someone should try to win the affection of someone else of interest. Too often, many within the body of Christ possess impure motives while witnessing. Thereby, the phrase "Do you know Jesus?" or "Maybe, we can have personal bible study together" become pick-up lines instead of a means to rescue someone from the clutches of hell.

2. It is not a means to acquire self-glory and prestige. I once met a group of people who were quite zealous for soul winning, but they kept tally each day of how many people they "led to the Lord" in a very competitive manner. It seemed that they were more concerned about who was the "better soul-winner," than simply doing the will of the Father. Jesus, the greatest evangelist of all time, indeed received notoriety; however, all glory went to God the Father.

    In fact, we are to *"Let [our] light so shine before men, that they may see your good works, and glorify your Father which is in heaven" (Matthew 5:16).* All Glory should go to our Heavenly Father (see 1 Corinthians 6:20 and 1 Corinthians 9:16-17).

3. It is not optional! *"Go ye therefore, and teach all nations, baptizing them in the name of the Father, and of the Son, and of the Holy Ghost: Teaching them to observe all things whatsoever I have commanded you: and, lo, I am with you always, even unto the end of the world. Amen" (Matthew 28:19-20).*

4. The aforementioned scripture is known as the Great Commission. Unfortunately, it has been said that it is the Great Omission because many believe that this commandment, spoken by Jesus himself, doesn't apply to them. If it does, witnessing is something to do if and when you feel like it. As a result, the Great Commission to evangelize the lost has been reduced to a mere suggestion and not a commandment.

5. It is not something that's reserved for the leadership of the church. Too often, the Body of Christ accepts lies from the devil that it's not my job to reach others for Christ. There are many who might say, *"I'll let Pastor, Evangelist, Minister or Deacon/ness So-and-So do it".* Besides, I'm not so great at this anyway! That thought is the furthest from the truth.

Evangelism Defined:

One translation put it this way: **Evangelism is teaching** (heralding, proclaiming, preaching) **the Gospel** (the message from God that leads us to salvation) **with the aim** (hope, desire, goal) **to persuade** (convince, convert).

The Strong's Concordance defines **an evangelist** *(G2009 euaggelistes from 2097)* **as a preacher of the Gospel.** *Euaggelizo from 2095 and 32;* **to announce good news** *("evangelize")* **especially the gospel:**--declare, **bring** (declare, show) **glad** (good) **tidings**, preach (the gospel).

The Vines Expository Dictionary defines evangelist (G2009 euangelistes) as **"a messenger of good"** *(eu, "well", angelos, "a messenger"),* **denotes a "preacher of the Gospel,"** *Acts 2:18; Ephesians 4:11,* **which makes clear the distinctiveness of the function in the churches;** *2 Timothy 4:5. Cp. Euangelizo,* **"to proclaim glad tidings,"** *and euangelion,* **"good news, gospel.**

The verses of scripture below refers to examples of what **"Glad Tidings"** and what the **"Good News"** are.

> *"But God commendeth his love toward us, in that, while we were yet sinners, Christ died for us." Romans 5:8*
>
> *"That if thou shall confess with thy mouth the Lord Jesus, and shalt believe in thine heart that God raised him from the dead, thou shalt be saved." Romans 10:9*
>
> *"For God so loved the world, that he gave his only begotten Son that whosoever believeth in him should not perish, but have everlasting life." John 3:16*
>
> *"Therefore if any man be in Christ, he a new creature: old things are passed away; behold, all things are become new." 2 Corinthians 5:17*
>
> *"If we confess our sins, he is faithful and just to forgive us our sins, and to cleanse us from all unrighteousness." 1 John 1:9*

Evangelism should also be...

1. Evangelism should be an honest account of what God has done or is presently doing overall and in one's own life.

If God delivered you from 1 pack of cigarettes a day, don't say He delivered you from 5 packs! While the temptation to embellish the truth is there because it might make our testimonies sound more appealing, there's no need to lie. When sharing the gospel, we are simply witnesses of God's power and workings in our lives. Should the Holy Spirit lead us to share our stories, remember that lying will short circuit the anointing while witnessing. It is the truth that makes people free, not fabricated stories (See John 8:32). Besides, **"a faithful witness will not lie"** (Proverbs 14:5). When the disciples evangelized, speaking of the things that they had both seen and heard, they always referred to themselves as witnesses: (See Acts 2:32, 3:15, 5:32, 10:39). The Apostle Paul gave a sincere account of his own encounter with Jesus on the Road to Damascus (See Acts 26:13).

2. Evangelism should be Spirit led (See Romans 8:14, Acts 8:26-38)

Phillip was in the midst of a red-hot revival in Samaria, when God through his angel led him 94 miles away to the Gaza Strip. First, Phillip had to be listening and receptive to the message. Second, he had to be willing to come out of his comfort zone. Most people would not be willing to leave in the middle of a revival. Third, he had to be obedient in order to approach the Ethiopian Eunuch when the **"Spirit said unto Philip, Go near, and join thyself to this chariot"** (Acts 8:29). Phillip took his queue from Jesus when they had traveled to Samaria in John chapter 4. It's important to note that the Samaritans were a mixed-breed of people from Jewish descent; their practices were laced with idolatry. Historically, the Jews and Samaritans had no dealings with each other. Nevertheless, the gospel message spread through Samaria. This means that racism had no place in the furtherance of the gospel. We should not be afraid to witness to people who look different from us or have a different socio-economic status than do we. (We will discuss this more in chapter 2.)

Moreover, Phillip, like the other apostles, was willing to hazard his life for the gospel. Though scriptures do not say this, we do not know how many Ethiopian guards were there to protect the Eunuch. It would be quite normal for a high-ranking official to have an entourage with him on such a long journey. Like today, coming too close to an official of such status could prove to be both risky and dangerous. No longer concerned about racial differences or social status, Phillip could be led to the prominent Ethiopian official because salvation was the priority.

3. Evangelism should bring conviction and repentance (See Acts 2:14-41)

People must see their need for a Savior while we're witnessing or evangelizing to them. Nowadays, there are many who preach "feel good" gospels about happiness, prosperity, peace and joy. Never do these messages make people accountable for their decisions, call out their sins, and cause them to make amends with the Holy God whom they've offended. The goal isn't to make people feel good about him/herself when sharing the gospel with them. Yes, we must share the truth in love. However, people shouldn't leave our presence feeling okay and secure in their sins. Instead, they should leave feeling convicted if they haven't yet received Christ.

Apart from being an apostle, Peter was also an evangelist. He preached the first evangelical message, and 3,000 souls were saved. (We'll discuss this more in chapter 5.) While Peter was full of the Holy Ghost, he preached the Word of God. Though Peter spoke the truth (Word of God) in love, *"they were pricked in their heart, and said unto Peter and the rest of the apostles, Men and brethren, what shall we do?"* (Acts 2:37). Sharing the truth in love will not always be warm and fuzzy. The Word of God exposes the sinful heart for what it is.

> *"For the word of God is quick, and powerful, and sharper than any two edged sword, piercing even to the dividing asunder of soul and spirit, and of the joints and marrow, and is a discerner of the thoughts and intents of the heart"* (Hebrews 4:12).

God's Word can go where we can't. Because God's Word is living, it can go into the inner crevices of the heart and shed light on sin. Thereby, the Holy Spirit convicts the hearer of his/her sin as we share the Word. Moreover, God's Word will not return unto Him void, but will accomplish everything He sends it to do (See Isaiah 55:11). It's like a boomerang being thrown to complete its intended task; then, it returns back to its sender. So it is with the Word of God. As a result, sharing God's word His way should bring Godly sorrow, which leads to repentance (See 2 Corinthians 7:10).

Jesus, the Evangelist
Jesus, the Living Word, was the Master evangelist! He constantly demonstrated the fundamentals of witnessing during his earthly ministry. Let's explore what He taught us in John Chapter 4 when he met the woman of Samaria.

What Jesus taught about evangelism through His ministry?
*Jesus was sensitive and discerning towards the Father's will because of a lifestyle of prayer and fasting. (John 4:4)
*Jesus sacrificed his own comforts to reach a soul. Though tired, thirsty and hungry, He pressed beyond his flesh. (John 4:6-8)
*Jesus demonstrated compassion, as He pressed beyond discrimination. (John 4:9)
*Jesus' lifestyle solidified everything he said. (John 4:16)
*Jesus was contagious! His evangelism caused others to evangelize. (John 4:25-29)
"...Come, see a man, which told me all things that I ever did; is not this the Christ?"

Chapter 1 Review

What Is Evangelism?

Chapter Theme

Historically many in the Body of Christ have had a narrow view concerning what evangelism is and who is to evangelize. Some associate evangelism with the job of women ministers who they do not want to address as ministers of the Gospel. Others, view it solely as an unimportant office for some individual but not a calling for every born-again believer.

This chapter looks at what evangelism is and what it is not so that you can come to the full knowledge of your calling and be equipped as a saint of the Lord. It will answer questions such as these: What does the word evangelize mean? What is evangelism and what it is not? What did Jesus teach by his life example about evangelism? Who is called to evangelize?

Questions For Reflection

1. How would you define Evangelism _____
_____
_____
_____
_____

2. Prior to reading this chapter, how have you been shaped by the common views you have heard or been taught regarding what evangelism is? _____
_____
_____
_____
_____

3. Are there any attitudes buried in your heart that have withheld you from sharing the Gospel with someone of another ethnic group? _____
_____
_____
_____
_____

4. Do you feel confused or unsure of what your role is concerning evangelism?
_____
_____
_____

Exploring God's Principles For Evangelism

1. List three things Evangelism is not _____, _____, _____.

2. Evangelism is teaching (heralding, proclaiming, preaching) the gospel (the message from God that leads us to _____), with the aim to _____ (convince, convert).

3. Evangelism should be a _____ account of what God has done or is presently doing overall and in one's own life.

4. Based on Romans 8:14 and Acts 8:26-38 evangelism should be led by _____.

Applying God's Principle For Evangelism

Thinking It Over
1. Who will be the recipient of hearing the Good News from your lips if you are lead by Holy Spirit?
_____
_____
_____

2. What have you learned from Jesus' example of evangelism with the Samaritan woman?
_____
_____
_____

3. What will you duplicate from Jesus and Phillip's example of evangelism?
_____
_____
_____

Praying About It
Repent for the ways you have made the Great Commission the Great Omission.

Pray that Holy Spirit will quicken your understanding about your God given mandate to evangelize the lost.

Ask God to create a clean heart in you to evangelize others no matter their ethnic group.

Acting On God's Truth
If you have had impure motives in your efforts to evangelize, search the scriptures and allow God's word to renew your mind.

How much consideration have you given to whether you are following in Jesus footstep to go out of your way to share the love of Christ.

Commit to memory Matthew 28:19 as a reminder that you are called to evangelize.

CHAPTER 2

GOAL OF EVANGELISM

"For the Son of man is come to seek and to save that which was lost." (Luke 19:10.) Yet, Christians often hesitate to reach out to those who are different. They want God to clean the fish before they catch them.

-Jim Cymbala-

What is The Goal of Evangelism?

Some may wonder why we are even discussing this topic. However, it's needful to make some things clear. The goal of evangelism is salvation. Salvation means to be rescued/saved by God from the consequences of our sin. It is simply a recognition that I have broken all of God's laws, deserve judgment for my sins, and can only be pardoned by the shed blood of Jesus Christ.

Motivation For Witnessing:
I've met people who witness just to witness, but they don't have a genuine expectation for souls to be saved while sharing the gospel. They do it because it's on the church calendar or on the list of things-to-do, but there really is no anticipation or belief that someone can be saved by their efforts. Have you ever seen a person who went fishing, baited the hook, put the pole in the water, and was shocked that he/she hooked a fish? I've seen it many times during our church fishing trips. The person would be so shocked that his or her pole started moving, and would panic saying, "oh my goodness, what do I do...what do I do? It's moving!" Likewise, there are many who are moved to conviction and repentance by Holy Spirit through our efforts, and we draw a blank regarding what to do next. It's simple! Ask him or her if he or she would like to invite Jesus Christ to be Lord and Savior of their life.

Others evangelize because they desire to appear noble before people, and/or they do it for the sake of saying, "Yeah, I witness all the time" if someone asks them. Even worse, many have a respect of persons while witnessing (see James 2:3). There are some people who deliberately target women, those who are affluent, or those appearing to have means because of ill motives. Jesus desires that we would be fishers of men as we follow Him. Let's not pick and choose which kind of fish we should be catching for Christ. This means that everyone is a prime candidate for salvation. These candidates include various ethnicities as mentioned earlier, young and old, rich and poor, gang bangers, drug users, drug dealers, homeless, prostitutes, pimps, those with alternate sexual lifestyles, alcoholics and others who many would steer clear from. Why would God want them? It's easy. He wants them for the same reason he wants you!

1 Corinthians 1:27-29 declares:
> *"But God hath chosen the foolish things of the world to confound the wise; and God hath chosen the weak things of the world to confound the things which are mighty; And base things of the world, and things which are despised, hath God chosen, yea, and things which are not, to bring to nought things that are: That no flesh should glory in his presence."*

In other words, God enjoys taking messy people and situations, cleaning them up, and making them new for His glory. Remember Jesus said, "...they that be whole need not a physician, but they that are sick" (Matthew 9:12). Furthermore, He loves using unconventional means and choosing the "least-likely" or "less-desirables" to accomplish His will in the earth. This happens so that the world could take note that only an awesome, mighty, and powerful God could do this! Amen.

Therefore, the ultimate goal and purpose of evangelism is salvation and discipleship. Many have need of salvation, while others may have made a decision for Christ without moving on to discipleship. Regardless, the Lord has commissioned us for a sacred task. Let us be diligent in completing it for Him!

Misunderstanding About Salvation:

Over the years, I have asked many sincere church-going people this exact question: What is Salvation? To my dismay, I've heard many answers like the following:

-When you go to church, read your Bible and try to live right.

-When you get baptized.

-I don't know; no one really broke it down for me.

This is very alarming. Very few said, accepting Jesus Christ as your Personal Lord and Savior. To those few, I then followed up with these questions:

-Lord of what? What does it mean for Jesus Christ to be your Lord?

-What does it mean for Jesus Christ to become your Savior? What is He saving you from?

-If I wanted to be saved or born-again, what would I have to do?

Unfortunately, people were stumped and looked puzzled; I could count on one hand over the years how many knew what Salvation was and could explain how to be saved by grace through faith in Jesus Christ (See Ephesians 2:8-9). How can we effectively communicate the gospel message of salvation if we're not quite sure what it is? It is no wonder why the Body of Christ is in trouble and that countless people are not being saved. Many have learned church etiquette or church culture, but they have not learned Christ (See Ephesians 4:20).

Personal Testimony

I was one of those sincere church-going people. I was in the church, involved in various ministries and yet I could not answer the questions above. Tired of the uncertainty, I asked my schoolmate what it meant and what to do to be saved. When we'd hung up the phone,

I prayed in my bedroom and asked Jesus to forgive me and come live in my heart. Finally, I felt relieved in knowing that I was saved. Though serving in a local body of believers is a necessity in the plan and purpose of God, I realized that doing all those works did not solidify my salvation. I could have died in my sins though I went to church faithfully, and no one told me? You might be surprised that there may be some in the pews of your church or involved in its decision-making, who may not be saved. Ask God for discernment and wisdom regarding how to approach them. By the way, I have led many churchgoers to invite Christ to be their Savior by asking the questions mentioned above.

Inviting Jesus Christ Into Your Heart:

Have you ever invited Jesus Christ to become your Personal Lord and Savior? That simply means that you have made Jesus Christ the Lord or "Master" of your life and have been "saved" from the penalty of your sins as well as from the wrath to come when Jesus returns. Salvation or the Rebirth occurs after a person confesses and repents of his/her sins to the Lord Jesus Christ; then, he or she sincerely asks Jesus to come and live inside his/her heart. From that moment on, the blood of Jesus Christ has washed the sins of that person away. Furthermore, that person is now a part of the family of God and Body of Christ.

> **1 John 1:9 says:** *"If we confess our sins, he is faithful and just to forgive us our sins, and to cleanse us from all unrighteousness."*

What's more? The Spirit of Christ, Himself, comes to indwell that person. Some people confuse Salvation or being Born-Again with Baptism. However, Baptism occurs after a person has received Christ as Lord and Savior. In and of itself, it isn't salvation. In fact, Baptism, on the other hand, is a public display of what took place in the Spirit realm. The symbolic cleansing by water is an outward demonstration of the spiritual cleansing that took place when a person got saved. I've encountered many who have been baptized, but they never recalled saying a Sinner's Prayer or Prayer of Salvation. A Sinner's Prayer is a short way of saying that a person has confessed Jesus Christ as the Son of God, believe in their heart that he rose from the dead, repent or turn away from their sins and receive God's forgiveness (See Roman's 10:9-10). A person, who has been baptized without sincerely saying a Sinner's Prayer, forfeits the benefits given to us through Salvation. God said in His Word that he has **"blessed us with all spiritual blessings in heavenly places in Christ"** (Ephesians 1:3). Nonetheless, going through the motions of Baptism only will not afford us those benefits. I've heard it said many times, that a person "can go down in the water a dry devil, and come back up a wet devil" because regeneration has not taken place! If you're not sure about your own salvation, please pray a prayer like the one below with your whole heart:

PRAY

Heavenly Father, I come to you admitting that I am a sinner.
I know I have done many terrible sins in your sight. I repent and

choose to turn away from all my sins. I ask that you cleanse me of all unrighteousness. Lord, I believe that Jesus is your Son and that He died on the cross for my sins. I also believe that He rose again from the dead on the third day so that I might be forgiven. I ask Jesus Christ to be my Lord and Savior today. I choose to follow and obey His Word. I ask for Holy Spirit to come into my life to lead and guide me into all truth. Thank you for saving me and making me your child, in Jesus' name Amen.

Whether you've said a prayer like this a few minutes ago or many years ago, I personally want to congratulate you on making the best decision of your life! Does this mean that you will be void of challenges, pain, and trials in your life? Absolutely not! That's absurd! I would be presenting a lop-sided gospel if I told you otherwise. The human experience is filled with them.

> *"These things I have spoken unto you, that in me ye might have peace. In the world ye shall have tribulation: but be of good cheer; I have overcome the world"*
> *(John 16:33).*

In fact, we are guaranteed troubled times, though many preach different gospel messages to satisfy the lusts and greed of this generation. Nevertheless, we are also guaranteed peace through the Prince of Peace himself. He would rather us have peace in the midst of our trials than to be in pieces. As a result, you and I can rest assured that we've made our reservations in heaven, and this present life is temporary. No matter the trial or hardship, we can be reminded that we are strangers passing through this cold, bitter world unto our final destination. While we're here, however, let's get busy for Jesus and bring as many people with us to heaven as possible. We were born for this. Even better, we were born-again for this!

Chapter 2 Review

The Goal Of Evangelism

Chapter Theme

Many people in the church and outside the church have improperly used the term "saved", "born again", and "new birth" without a clear understanding of what these terms mean. They often confuse salvation with baptism. Therefore, they are limited in seeing the necessity and value of evangelism, which leads to salvation.

This chapter emphasizes the principle and primary reason for evangelism, which is for the salvation of men/women. Salvation is received when a sinner confesses Jesus Christ as the Son of God, believes in his/her heart that he rose from the dead, repents or turns away from his/her sins and receives God's forgiveness. This chapter answers the following questions. What is salvation? What is Baptism? How do you receive salvation?

Questions For Reflection

1. How would you define salvation?
_____
_____
_____

2. Can you be a child of God with reservations in heaven without salvation?
_____
_____
_____

3. Is it reasonable to believe that being a good churchgoer is a prerequisite for going to heaven?
_____
_____
_____

Exploring God's Principles For The Goals Of Evangelism

1. The goal of evangelism is _____.

2. Salvation means to be _____ from the penalty of _____.

3. Baptism is a _____ display of what took place in the _____ realm.

4. The symbolic cleansing by water is an _____ demonstration of the _____ cleansing that took place when a person got saved.

5. A Sinner's Prayer is a short way of saying that a person has, _____ Jesus Christ as the Son of God, _____ in their heart that he rose from the dead, _____ or turn away from their sins and receive God's forgiveness.

Applying God's Principle For The Goals Of Evangelism

Thinking It Over
When Jesus returns, what would happen to you if all you did was attend church services, participate on the various auxiliaries, and was baptized?

_____
_____
_____

Do you remember inviting Jesus Christ to become your Personal Lord and Savior?
Will troubles be a deterrent to you receiving God's salvation if you haven't already?

_____
_____
_____
_____

Praying About It
Ask the Lord to forgive you for any misconception you've had concerning baptism and salvation.
If you have not previously invited Jesus Christ to be your personal Lord and Savior take time now to pray your own sinners' prayer.

Acting On God's Truth
Share your salvation experience with someone.
Memorize Ephesians 2:8-9 to help you remember a clear definition of what salvation is.

CHAPTER 3:
YOUR DUTY TO EVANGELIZE

"While it is true that God gifts some for ministry as evangelists, He calls all believers to be His witnesses and provides them with both the power to witness and a powerful message...Just as each Christian, regardless of spiritual gift or ministry, is to love others, so each believer is to evangelize..."

-David S. Whitney

Why is Evangelism Our Duty?

Let us begin by defining what duty means. The English Oxford dictionary defines duty as a moral or legal obligation; a responsibility. It can also be viewed as a task or action that someone is required to perform. There are four duties that we would like to explore as it relates to evangelism.

1. It is Our God-given mandate and responsibility.

> *"But ye shall receive power, after that the Holy Ghost is come upon you: and ye shall be witnesses unto me both in Jerusalem, and in all Judaea, and in Samaria, and unto the uttermost part of the earth" (See Acts 1:8).*

Please notice that the aforementioned scripture says, "shall be witnesses," not might be. The implication here is that this mandate is non-negotiable. The Lord never asked us if we wanted to do this or not. The question is: have you received power from the Holy Ghost? We are responsible to receive the Holy Ghost. This will determine our level of effectiveness and our sphere of influence.

2. It is Our Reasonable Service.

> *"I beseech you therefore, brethren, by the mercies of God, that ye present your bodies a living sacrifice, holy, acceptable unto God, which is your reasonable service" (Romans 12:1).*

Evangelism, itself, is sacrificial in nature. Why? Pulling people out of the fire entails that we must be willing to endure the heat of the flames in order to rescue someone from it (See Jude 1:22-23). However, what's awesome about God is that He will never ask us to do anything that is unreasonable. He first set the example by sending Jesus Christ as a sacrifice for us all.

Second, the Lord equipped us with the necessary tools when we accepted Him by **"bless[ing] us with all spiritual blessings in heavenly places in Christ"** (Ephesians 1:3). Third, any seemingly insurmountable feat is conquerable because we **"can do all things through Christ who strengthens [us]"** (Philippians 4:13). That's pretty fair!

3. It is Our Ministry.

> *"Therefore if any man be in Christ, he is a new creature: old things are passed away; behold, all things are become new. And all things are of God, who hath reconciled us to himself by Jesus Christ, and hath given to us the ministry of reconciliation;*

To wit, that God was in Christ, reconciling the world unto Himself, not imputing their trespasses unto them; and hath committed unto us the word of reconciliation" (2 Corinthians 5:17-19).

Have you ever asked yourself after you received Jesus Christ as your personal Lord and Savior "what is my calling or my ministry? What do I do now?" Well, I have great news for you!! No matter if you just got saved today or if you've been saved for decades, we all have the ministry of reconciliation. Hallelujah!! What's reconciliation, you might ask? Webster's dictionary defines reconciliation as the means to restore to friendship, harmony or to settle and resolve a situation of conflict.

That means that we have been reborn, or Born-Again with a new purpose. That purpose is to point people past us and to God on a daily basis. Everything about us should give God glory to that end. In other words, our ministry or service of reconciliation is to bring the lost/unsaved back in harmony with God the Father.

When God created Adam and Eve in the Garden of Eden, the Lord created them after his similitude to have fellowship, friendship, and harmony with Him. They could walk and talk with Him in the cool of the day freely. Satan, the Great Deceiver acted as that jealous third party between God and humankind. His attitude was: If I can't go back to heaven, no one else can! After much enticement from the devil, they sinned, and the fellowship and harmony between God and man had been broken because our sins separate us from God (see Isaiah 59:2). From that time to the present, every human being was born with a sin-nature with reservations for hell.

Witnessing or evangelism seeks to allow God to use us in order to settle or resolve the issue between God and mankind. The unconverted soul is estranged to God; therefore, there is a desperate need for a mediator and advocate to bring us back in harmony with God the Father. Nevertheless, there's only one way to do so. The Bible declares: **"Jesus saith unto him, I am the way, the truth, and the life: no man cometh unto the Father, but by me"** (John 14:6).

Thankfully, Jesus is the one who bridges the gap between God and sinful mankind. This allows all humanity to be delivered from that old sin nature, only if they believe and receive the free gift of salvation. Since we are saved, it is our duty and ministry to bring all whom we encounter into the saving knowledge of Jesus Christ.

4. It Is The Means In Which We Build God's Kingdom

Zechariah 8:23 says the following: **"Thus saith the Lord of hosts; In those days it shall come to pass, that ten men shall take hold out of all languages of the nations, even shall take hold of the skirt... saying, We will go with you: for we have heard that God is with you".**

If you're not going to church anywhere, where will they follow you? As those who are saved or born again, we are required by God to attend church faithfully (See Hebrews 10:25). Even if you are a traveling evangelist or minister, you should be accountable to a local body of believers that will keep you covered in prayer with your evangelistic endeavors. Seek God in order to lead you to the right place. While no church is perfect, there is a church that's just right for you.

If you haven't done so already, find a local church in which to grow and serve. This may sound silly, but it must be addressed! I've encountered many Christians, who go through great, pain-staking lengths to evangelize, which is quite admirable. Nevertheless, when the hearer/s are ready and willing to commit to Jesus and follow them to church, these particular Christians say, "Oh, I don't go to church. I worship at home" or "I do my own thing." This is both detrimental to the potential convert as well as the one who's witnessing.

Furthermore, faithful church attendance is necessary to the development of the Christian walk and essential to evangelism. This also applies to those who are inconsistent in church attendance. After all, it's silly to invite someone to church and you, yourself, not be present because of some trivial reason. Think about what message we send about the church and our salvation if we're not faithfully attending when they come. Please note: This assertion does not apply to those who faithfully attend church, while giving recommendations to sinners of local churches in their respective areas to consider.

Moreover, we are also expected to use our time, talents, gifts, resources and skills for the building up of the Kingdom of God. Wouldn't that be considered "works," Margaret? No, our salvation ***"is the gift of God: Not of works, lest any man should boast"*** (Ephesians 2:8-9). We evangelize out of appreciation for the gift of salvation, not to work to earn it. Our gratitude should be expressed to God for the work that Christ has done on the cross. It is solely because of God's grace that we do what we do. We must also pray and read our Bibles daily. This may sound rudimentary, but I attended a church for years that never encouraged personal Bible reading and studying; in fact, we read the

Bibles in the back of the pews only during Sunday service alone. Again, it is important to stress that we do not work or serve to earn heaven, and we must be careful to relay that message to the unconverted soul.

Chapter 3 Review
Your Duty To Evangelize

Chapter Theme
This chapter emphasizes our duty to evangelize. Oftentimes many people confuse duty

with works. Our duty is an act of appreciation of what God has done for us. Therefore, we commit ourselves to partner with Christ to win souls, and present them to the Father. This is not a work in which we earn or get a payment for our labor. We do not seek to fulfill our duty as a means to get a reward of going to heaven when we die or as a means to gain favor with God. Salvation is a free gift. We work because we are saved, not as a means to be saved.

Questions For Reflection

1. Define duty?
___
___
___

2. Have you developed any misunderstanding about your duty to evangelize from previous teachings you received?
___
___
___

3. Do you feel any confusion or frustration about what your duty and responsibility should be concerning evangelism?
___
___
___

4. In what ways have you shunned your duty to evangelize?
___
___
___

Exploring God's Principles In Our Duty To Evangelize

1. The duty of evangelism is our _____ and _____.

2. Our duty to evangelize is _____ in nature.

3. According to 2 Corinthians 5:17, we have been given the ministry or duty of _____, which means we point people to Jesus every day.

4. Since we are saved, it is our duty and ministry to bring all whom we encounter into the _____ of Jesus Christ.

Applying God's Principle In Our Duty To Evangelize

Thinking It Over
1. What have you learned about your duty to reconcile man to God?
_____
_____
_____

2. Who will follow in your footstep to go to the house of God?
_____
_____
_____

Praying About It
1. Pray that Holy Spirit stir up the ministry of evangelism in you.

2. Repent for the way you have ignored, disobeyed or failed in fulfilling your duty to evangelize.

3. Ask God to cause you to be sensitive to the needs of those he puts you in the midst of who need to hear the Gospel message.

Acting on God's Truth
1. Memorize Romans 12:1 as a reminder that it is your duty or reasonable service to evangelize the lost.

2. Daily seek opportunities to make Christ known wherever you go.

3. Attend Church regularly as an example to others who would be prone to forsake assembling themselves with other believers.

CHAPTER 4:

THE ROLE OF THE EVANGELIST

"The Gospel is only good news if it gets there in time."

-Carl F.H. Henry

The Role Of The Evangelist

The role of the evangelist can be paralleled to the Paramedic. While the roles of EMS/EMT's and Paramedics vary from place to place, we will use the term Paramedics for all intensive purposes. Before we begin, please note that it is important to reiterate that we all are evangelists and have the ministry of reconciliation. This parallel isn't just for those who hold the office of an evangelist in the five-fold ministry alone, but it is for everyone who has received Jesus Christ as Lord and Savior. Now, let's consider the similarities:

1. They both must stay connected to their dispatcher to receive directions. Our dispatcher is Holy Spirit. Without staying connected to Holy Spirit, we go through the rat race of life listlessly, while hoping to positively encounter someone for Christ. Can you imagine Paramedics on an ambulance with a broken radio to their dispatcher? How effective could they possibly be for the facility or institution they represent? Our efforts will be just as futile if we do likewise. Let's think about it: if we do encounter someone, we're so undiscerning that we don't realize when we've had a God-ordained encounter. Nevertheless, if we do realize a God-ordained encounter, we would be clueless regarding what to say or do because we aren't connected to the True Vine.

> *"Abide in me, and I in you. As the branch cannot bear fruit of itself, except it abide in the vine; no more can ye, except ye abide in me. I am the vine, ye are the branches: He that abideth in me, and I in him, the same bringeth forth much fruit: for without me ye can do nothing" (John 15:4-5).*

According to Strong's Concordance, "abide" in this text, means to stay in a given place, state, relation or expectancy. It also means to remain, dwell, continue, and endure.

How do we do that? We abide by reading, studying, fasting, and meditating on God's Word. Most importantly, we do so by constant prayer/communication with Him (we'll discuss prayer more in depth later). If we don't abide in Him, we will have lost many opportunities to witness for him and realized it when it is much too late. In retrospect, there were so many missed opportunities for witnessing in my life, and I realized it after the fact because I wasn't properly abiding in Christ during those seasons of my life.

Moreover, people can be right in our midst while at work, home, church, and in our travels. They could be pacing back and forth at work, telling us their problems, having anxiety attacks in our midst, waiting impatiently in line near us at a grocery store or bank, crying as they're reading a text message, and the list goes on. Nonetheless, we will be ineffective if we've lost our connection.

Can the Paramedics really do a stellar job of knowing when and where to go with a lost signal or a broken walky-talky? Failure to report, replace, or immediately address such issues could cost lives. The same is true of us as Christians.

Like the Paramedic, it's a dire emergency and necessity for us as Christians to maintain a proper connection with Holy Spirit. Should we do so, we will be discerning enough to realize all the God-ordained encounters in our lives when we are abiding in Christ. Additionally, we will also be alert to know who's ripe for the picking and how to approach them.

2. They are both First Responders!

Like the emergency response worker, the evangelist understands that each situation is urgent. Every minute counts! According to The Gospel Coalition (TGC), the following numbers are startling!

    105 people die each minute.
    6,316 people die each hour.
    151, 600 people die each day.
    55.3 million people die each year.

By the time you finish reading this chapter, think about how many people will have already died. It's no wonder why we are to be "redeeming the time because the days are evil" (Ephesians 5:16).

Believe it or not, there are thousands or perhaps millions of people who are waiting for you to tell them about Jesus and His gift of salvation. I've once heard it said that hell will be filled with sinners who are angry with Christians because we never told them. Due to the moral decay and spiritual depravity all around us, people are looking for hope.

> ***The Bible says this: "Put ye in the sickle, for the harvest is ripe: come, get you down for the press is full…for their wickedness is great. Multitudes, multitudes in the valley of decision: for the day of the Lord is near in the valley of decision" (Joel 3:14).***

Will people "in the valley of decision" choose Christ because of your urgency for souls today? Let's continue on with the Emergency response team. The ideal time for the Paramedic workers to arrive on the scene is 8 minutes. Though unfortunate, it's understood that in many settings this is not adhered to.

I once saw a story on the news about a large city in the United States, which had an average response time of 18-27 minutes for the Paramedics to arrive on the scene. The rationale for this travesty was that there simply weren't enough ambulatory units or vehicles, and there wasn't enough staffing because of budget cuts. As a result, these workers were forced to drive 30-50 miles across town to go from one emergency to the next. Can you imagine how many fatalities there must have been? Can you imagine how many people slipped away in those extra minutes?

Could you fathom the heartbreak and disappointment of family members or onlookers who were on the scene?

Dear Reader, this scenario is a reminder of what Jesus said in Matthew 9:38-39.

> *"...The harvest truly is plenteous, but the labourers are few; Pray therefore the Lord of the harvest, that He will send forth more labourers into His harvest."*

The "Labourers" could certainly use your help! Are you willing?

I recently came across a true story that drove it home for me. There was a certain river in South Asia. Worshippers consider this river to be sacred, and they believe that they can find healing and forgiveness there. It's quite normal to throw ashes of the dead into the river with hopes of obtaining blessings from the deceased. People also wash in this river, presenting their wants and needs to the gods.

One day, a man deliberately went to the river to tell people how they could find healing and forgiveness in Christ. As he approached, he heard a horrible weeping and wailing of this one particular woman, who was beating her chest in grief. The woman told the Christian man that her husband had tuberculosis and had been out of work for a long time. Their hope was gone. "The troubles in my home are so great" she said, "and my sins are so many, so I gave the best I had to offer: my first born son."

The man was horror struck when he learned that she had thrown her baby into the river as an offering to the gods. As tears streamed down his face, the man told her how she could receive forgiveness through Jesus Christ. "Why couldn't you have come a half-hour sooner?" she asked in anguish. "Then I would not have sacrificed my son" *(Yohanan, Living in the Light of Eternity, Gospel for Asia Books).* Time is running out. Let's be about the Father's business today.

3. The Paramedic and evangelist both have to assess the situation on the scene.
We have probably seen on TV or real life how the emergency response worker asks a series of questions to the patient or those nearby to assess the severity of the matter and the responsiveness of the patient. In Isaiah Chapter 1, the Bible talks about sin-sickness. Likewise the evangelist must also ask questions to assess how deeply rooted in sin-sickness the potential convert is, while discerning what spirits are at work in a person's life. This discernment can only be acquired through Holy Spirit.

Quite often, we're too busy talking, and we don't do enough listening. We should be listening to the Holy Spirit as well as the person. If you listen well enough, the person will tell you just how to witness to him/her. Moreover, I caution you not to judge the book by its cover! Otherwise, you will damage a person if you do.

4. The Paramedic and the evangelist both have to give the right treatment at the right time, safely and appropriately.
For the evangelist, this requires **"rightly dividing the Word of Truth."** (2 Timothy 2:15)

Nevertheless, it's hard to divide something you don't know or haven't studied! If you don't know much scripture, use what you do know; however, continually read the Word of God daily. Set aside time to "study to show yourself approved unto God." Jeremiah put it this way: ***"Thy words were found, and I did eat them; and thy word was unto me the joy and rejoicing of mine heart: for I am called by thy name, O Lord God of hosts" (Jeremiah 15:16).***

In other words, anything we eat or consume gets in our bloodstream. The same is true spiritually. Let's eat the Word of God and become so filled that we get it in our bloodstream. Then, let it ooze from our pours as we witness! Holy Spirit will bring to mind the proper scripture/s for any given occasion as you yield to Him.

More specifically, know the 10 Commandments of God, which are also considered the law. You may be saying to yourself, "but aren't we under grace, Margaret?" Yes, but the law of God is our "schoolmaster", teaching us how sinful we are in light of God's Word. It shows us how we've offended God and our desperate need for salvation (See Galatians 3:24). Why? Because ***"the law of the Lord is perfect, converting the soul... the commandment of the Lord is pure, enlightening the eyes" (Psalms 19:7-8).***

Application:
I've had plenty of conversations that sounded like this:

Me: Hi there! Could I give you a Christian tract and invite you to church?
Jane Doe: No I'm good. I'm spiritual already.
Me: Really? What makes you so good? What makes you so spiritual?
Jane D.: Well, I don't go to church, but my grandfather was a pastor, and my mom is a minister. I believe in the Creator, but I can read the Bible on my own. Besides, I haven't murdered anyone, and I give to charitable organizations.
Me: Have you ever stolen anything, even if it were a paper clip from someone's desk?
Jane D.: no.
Me: Ok, have you ever told a lie, even if it was a little white lie?
Jane D.: Yes.
Me: Have you ever looked at anyone to lust after him or her?
Jane D.: Wait, but that's normal! He was really fine; all the ladies wanted him! I mean, I'm really not that kind of girl! But...
Me: Please answer the question.
Jane D.: Yes.
Me: Have you ever used the Lord's name in vain or said any curse words?
Jane D.: yes.
Me: One last question. Have you ever hated anyone?
Jane D.: (She starts to look uneasy, and gets fidgety.) Yes, but... you don't know what that person did to me.
Me: Thanks Jane for your time! By your own admission you're a lying, adulterous, blasphemer, who's a murderer at heart. It sounds like you're not as good as you thought.

Jane D.: I understand the lying part, but how am I all those other things? The Bible says: ***"thou shalt not judge!"***
Me: According to the Bible, it says that whosoever looks upon someone to lust after him or her has already committed adultery with that person in his or her heart. Also, the Bible says, ***"Thou shalt not take the name of the Lord thy God in vain for the Lord will not hold him guiltless that taketh his name in vain" (Exodus 20:7).*** You've already admitted that you've done that.
Lastly, the Bible says that ***"Whosoever hateth his brother is a murderer: and ye know that no murderer hath eternal life abiding in him" (1 John 3:15).*** So it turns out that you are a murderer after all. If you were to stand before the Righteous Judge with the 10 commandments as the law, would you be innocent or guilty?
Jane D.: (looking troubled, she hesitates and whispers...) Guilty.
Me: I was guilty also, but these are the provisions that God made through his Son, Jesus Christ, for you and I.

Then, I emphasize the "Good News" that she doesn't have to stay in the spiritual state she's in by accepting the gift of Salvation. Next I ask, "would you like to invite Jesus Christ to be your Lord and Savior?" Usually, people will not repent if they don't see a need to do so. It is our job to show them what they look like in the mirror of God's Word. Letting the "commandment of the Lord enlighten their eyes," will cause them to see their desperate need for the Savior of the World. Again, they won't repent if we don't show them their need to do so.

5. They both have the ultimate purpose of saving lives.

> *"And of some have compassion, making a difference: And others save with fear, pulling them out of the fire; hating even the garment spotted by the flesh" (Jude 22-23).*

Paramedic workers don't show up on the scene, ask questions, and apply some form of treatment for good measure. Instead, they arrive already having intentions to save a life. Why? This is because it's their vocation. They signed up for this! The Apostle Paul said the following: ***"I, therefore the prisoner of the Lord, beseech you that ye walk worthy of the vocation wherewith ye are called..." (Ephesians 4:1).*** When you became a Born-Again Christian, you signed up for this! The awesome part is that it's a noble vocation that many will benefit from, so walk worthy of it.

6. They both rush people to the hospital to receive further treatment before it's too late.
One might assume that the evangelist does no such thing; however, I beg to differ! The Bible-believing, Holy Spirit-filled church where sound doctrine is preached is the hospital. This can be your church or another Word-church that's closer in proximity to him/her. ***Please note: Everyone you lead to Christ may not attend your church, and that's fine. Instead, the focus should be on the person going to a church where he or she can receive the Word of life.***

Also, there are times when a person may not accept the gift of salvation on the spot; if that happens, try earnestly to get the potential convert in the presence of God. Then, let Holy Spirit take care of the rest. As the spiritual paramedic, the evangelist rushes the spiritually wounded or dying through the Emergency Room (E.R.) then the Operating Room (O.R.) of the church for the doctor to operate on him/her.

The doctor isn't the pastor, the apostle, the deacon, or minister. The Doctor is Jesus himself! He alone is the Balm in Gilead and Jehovah Raphah (The Lord Who Heals You).
The ministerial staff and the body of believers in that local church are there to help the patient on the road to recovery by leading him/her to Christ and teaching the new convert to walk in his or her new God-given identity in Christ.

Chapter 4 Review

The Role of The Evangelist

Chapter Theme

This chapter parallels the role of the evangelist with the role of the Paramedics.
This section futher provides a clear view and detailed resume of the role of the evangelist. Questions about your personal role to evangelize will be answered through the scriptures.

Contrary to what some Christians believe, the role and work of the evangelist is everyone's ministry to reconcile men to Christ. Only through the help of Holy Spirit can you discern the spiritual emergencies of people, assess their spiritual needs, dispense the right treatment, and lead them to receiving spiritual health from Christ. He alone is the great physician healer.

Questions For Reflection

1. Have you missed opportunities to evangelize because you were not sensitive or discerning to the prompting of Holy Spirit?

_____
_____

2. How has your belief about the role of the evangelist impacted your response to lost souls?
_____
_____
_____

3. What would the outcome be for a person who was holding unto a window ledge of a burning building if you waited for a convenient opportunity or the right time to share the Gospel?
_____
_____
_____

4. How would you feel if you had a dyer medical emergency, and the Paramedic showed up 27 minutes after you called for help?
_____
_____
_____

5. What would you say or think of the Paramedic who arrived on the scene 27 minutes after you called for help? _____
_____
_____
_____

6. From the responses you provided above, can those same characteristics and responses be said of you from an evangelistic standpoint? Why or Why not?
_____
_____
_____

Exploring God's Principles For Salvation

1. When we abide in Christ by _____, studying, _____, and _____ on God's Word, we will prepare our self for a God-ordained encounter with sinners.

2. The evangelist must ask questions to assess how deep rooted in _____ the potential convert is while _____, what spirits are at work in the person's life?

3. The law of God is our _____, teaching us how sinful we are in light of God's Word, thereby revealing our desperate need for salvation.

Applying God's Principle For Salvation

Thinking It Over

1. What have you learned about the goal of the evangelist when parallel to the Paramedic?

_____
_____
_____

2. Is your response time to the spiritual dying around you reasonable to rescue them from the fires of hell?

_____
_____
_____

3. Can you be a follower of Jesus Christ in word or deed if you make no effort to evangelize the dying?

_____
_____
_____

Praying About It

1. Repent for your slothfulness, unpreparedness and busyness that cause you to be unavailable to direct someone to the Balm of Gilead.

2. Pray for yourself and other believers to have an evangelistic mindset to discern the needs of sinners and be quick to respond to them.

3. Ask God to send you as a laborer into the field to gather the harvest for Him.

Acting on God's Truth

1. Write down Jude 22-23 and memorize it as a reminder of your goal to evangelize.

2. What things will you do this week to share the Gospel with someone?

3. Count how many ambulances you see in your travels this week, and let it be a reminder of the urgency for souls to be saved.

CHAPTER 5:

HINDRANCES TO WITNESSING

"It is a serious reflection for the Evangelist that wherever God's Spirit is at work, there Satan is sure to be busy. We must remember and ever be prepared for this. The enemy of Christ and the enemy of souls is always on the watch, always hovering about to see what he can do, either to hinder or corrupt the work of the gospel. This need not terrify or even discourage the workman; but it is well to bear it in mind and be watchful. Satan will leave no stone unturned to mar or hinder the blessed work of God's Spirit. He has proved himself the ceaseless, vigilant enemy of that work, from the days of Eden down to the present moment."

- C.H. Mackintosh-

While on this journey of developing a lifestyle of evangelism, Satan will not sit idly by, and watch you enjoy your ministry of reconciliation. Instead, he will strategically place some of the following distractions in your midst to prevent you from witnessing and/or slowly cause you to lose your excitement for soul-winning.

1. Fear:

"For God hath not given us the spirit of fear; but of power, and of love, and of a sound mind" (2 Timothy 1:7).

If more people believed this scripture as it relates to evangelism, there would be a revival like never before. Though we are living in time of great persecution for the church, God is still providing opportunities to advance His kingdom. The hindrance of fear paralyzes many Christians today because they are consumed with whether or not they will say the right words in the right way.

When Jesus sent out the disciples in two's, He *"... commanded them that they should take nothing for their journey, save a staff only; no scrip, no bread, no money in their purse"* (Mark 6:8). Why would Jesus command such a thing? He did this so that the disciples could solely rely on God for the success of their mission. Like the disciples, our dependence must be on Holy Spirit only. It's not in our own abilities to be an effective witness for Christ. As we abide in the True Vine through fasting and praying, we will be emboldened by His Holy Spirit to accomplish the task at hand. We'll take a closer look at the importance of prayer later on in the chapter.

In addition, we must remember that we are only the messengers. If a U.P.S. carrier rings your doorbell to present you with a package, you have the option to accept or decline the package. The carrier doesn't break down and cry if you decline; instead, the worker simply says O.K., goes back to his truck, and finishes delivering the rest of his packages. The carrier doesn't beat himself up and wallow in self-pity, nor convince himself that he's the worst delivery guy who ever lived.

Should you find yourself in a situation when you are bringing someone the "Good News" package of eternal life through Jesus Christ and he/she declines, politely shake the dust off your feet and move on to the next delivery? Why? We are only held responsible for our actions, not the potential recipient's. Mulling over questions like, "What will he/she say if I tell him or her about Jesus? Will my responses be good enough or quick enough?" will hinder us from being the effective soul winners that God intended for us to be. Furthermore, such questions are ultimately designed by Satan to get us to talk ourselves out of witnessing altogether.
Guess what else? You might be relieved to know that you don't have to know all the answers!

Yes. We should **"study to shew [ourselves] approved unto God..."** (2 Timothy 2:15) as the Bible instructs; however, there are those who want us to stumble by asking questions like: why do babies die? Or why do good people die young? Most often, questions like those are intended to trip us up as opposed to causing the other person to come under conviction and saving faith in Jesus Christ.

The Bible says it best in 2 Timothy 2:16, 23: **"...shun vain and profane babblings: for they will increase unto more ungodliness. But foolish and unlearned questions avoid, knowing that they do gender strifes."**

If you find yourself in a situation like that, politely tell the person that you don't know the answers. However, let him/her know the service times at your church; once he/she comes, tell the potential convert that the right person on the ministerial staff can lead you on a quest to help you find the answers to your questions.

Perhaps, fear grips the heart of many believers, as they are often nervous or afraid of the receivers' response. We may find ourselves with sweaty palms, stuttering, or clearing our throats when looking at a person's facial expressions. Dear Reader, please understand that facial expressions are not always an indication of how a person may receive Christ. While you're sharing the "Good News" a person may have a mean look on his or her face. That does not always mean that the Gospel message will be rejected. Rather, this listener could be processing all that's being said. Moreover, This candidate for salvation also may be under the deep conviction of Holy Spirit as she/he considers his or her ways.

Maybe, Satan will try to get you to compare yourself to others who are witnessing for Christ, causing you to feel as though you are inadequate because you don't witness like others. You are not supposed to witness like them; you are suppose to witness like Christ. Though Jesus is God the Son, His effectiveness solely relied upon the time that he spent in constant prayer and communication with God the Father.

2. Inconsistency:

"For he that wavereth is like a wave of the sea driven with the wind and tossed. For let not that man think that he shall receive any thing of the Lord" (James 6b-7).

We often demonstrate what we believe by our behavior. If our behavior is inconsistent with the Word of God and more consistent with worldliness, then I can almost guarantee that people won't follow you to Jesus. Perhaps, people may humor you and come to church here and there, but they won't come to Jesus. There's a difference.

Though this may sound harsh, it calls for some serious introspection if we really want to be Kingdom-builders for God. We should be building God's Kingdom, not our own. In other words, are you quick tempered? Are you up one day and down the next? Are you known for gossiping? Do you use profanity? Do you tell off-colored jokes?

Are you lustful? Do you stir up strife or cause division at work or in the house of God? Do you fornicate just a little bit? Are you a complainer? Do you always look for the worst in people? Do you only read your Bible sometimes? Do you only pray sometimes? Do you tell a few little white lies here and there? Do you cheat people in any way? Do you put others down to make yourself look good? The list goes on and on.

One might say, "Hey, no body's perfect!" While this is true, it is quite unfortunate that many use this excuse as a license to sin. We should demonstrate consistent lifestyles that glorify the Father. Jesus said, **"And I, if I be lifted up from the earth, will draw all men unto me"** (John 12:32). With every decision you make ask yourself this: will Christ be lifted up in this? If others around us cannot tell that we are striving to be like Christ, we may be sending conflicting messages and damage those who are watching us.

In all things shewing thyself a pattern of good works: in doctrine shewing uncorruptness, gravity, sincerity, Sound speech, that cannot be condemned; that he that is of the contrary part may be ashamed, having no evil thing to say of you (Titus 2:7-8).

Every pattern shows consistency, or else it's not a pattern. If you have found yourself guilty of anything mentioned above, repent and ask God to cleanse you from these sins. Understand that true repentance is turning away from sin, so don't wait! Start anew today, and walk in your new identity in Christ. Others are depending on it!

3. Secret- Sins:

> *"Therefore seeing we have this ministry, as we have received mercy, we faint not; But have renounced the hidden things of dishonesty, not walking in craftiness, nor handling the word of God deceitfully; but by manifestation of the truth commending ourselves to every man's conscience in the sight of God. But if our gospel be hid, it is hid to them that are lost:"*(2 Corinthians 4:1-3).

You might be wondering what this has to do with witnessing. According to the scripture mentioned above, there's a direct correlation between the hidden sins in our lives and our level of effectiveness while sharing the gospel. They could range from laziness and unforgiveness to bitterness and envying.

We cannot renounce something that we haven't confessed and repented to the Lord. Otherwise, the renunciation is null and void. Rather, it becomes a form of godliness as we deny God's power to cleanse and deliver us from those sins (See 2 Timothy 3:5). Our goal should be to live a life of purity in thought, talk, and walk to allow our witnessing to become a lifestyle instead of words only. When we deviate from that by harboring pet sins in our hearts and practicing them on a consistent basis without having sincerely repented and turned from them, we short-circuit the power and anointing of Holy Spirit in our lives.

4. Sexual Sins

If you practice fornication, adultery, pornography, masturbation, or any other act of sexual perversion, you may have opened up a gateway to satanic influences in ways that you may not have intended. These influences will increase lustful impulses and take away from your message. If you have allowed yourself to indulge in these acts and have never repented, you've also allowed demonic influences to attach themselves to you. As a result, when you are praying with others, those demonic spirits get transferred to others. Consequently, the recipients also start to have the same sinful impulses with which you struggle. Whether you see them ever again, or you see them frequently, don't be quick to physically touch and agree with people in prayer and thereby pass on whatever spiritual influences that keep you or them in bondage because God will hold each and every one of us accountable.

Unfortunately, I have met different people who I have tried witnessing to; though they seemed receptive, there was this wall of resistance. Some of these included women who seemed like they would be such great candidates for salvation, but they shunned the gospel. As I tried getting down to the bottom of it, I asked this one young woman who I saw repeatedly, "why won't you accept Jesus as your Lord and Savior? You know scripture and get excited during conversations about God; most of all, you know that He is drawing you?" Her response broke my heart when she said this:

"I made a verbal confession to accept Jesus years ago, but the gentlemen that led me to Christ wound up fornicating with me. It made things complicated. I'm not so sure that I believe in [Christ] any more. He said that he repented and felt badly about it, but he wanted to still be in touch and have a relationship with me. I forgave him, but I'm searching out other religions now..."

Though I pleaded and pleaded with her about her soul, it was to no avail. Quite similarly, I was witnessing to a college buddy, who I had invited to church. His response sounded all too familiar. He looked me square in the eye saying, "honestly, Margaret... all the women who've invited me to church, I've already slept with... well, with the exception of you of course!" Hallelujah, that I broke his winning streak!! However, I caution you not to use witnessing as a tool to get to know someone a little better, with the motives of being intimate with them. Please bear in mind that God does not take that lightly.

Dear Friend: If you find that you have opened yourself up to various satanic influences and have allowed the devil to creep in, be honest with yourself. Confess your faults to the Lord, repent, and ask for His cleansing and deliverance in your life. Let's take a look at King David. In Psalm 51, David never blamed Bathsheba for bathing outside or looking so good. Instead, he was honest, took ownership of his actions, and humbly confessed his faults as he saw his own wretchedness.

It was then that he could ask God for change, saying.

> *"Create in me a clean heart, O God; and renew a right spirit within me. Cast me not away from thy presence; and take not thy holy spirit from me. Restore unto me the joy of thy salvation; and uphold me with thy free spirit. Then will I teach transgressors thy ways; and sinners shall be converted unto thee"* (Psalm 51:10-13).

Consequently, this change would reach far beyond him, causing sinners to also experience a transformation because of his self-examination and sincere repentance. David realized the privilege and power of prayer, thereby seizing the opportunity to make amends with God Almighty and be a tool to transform others' lives.

5. Self-Condemnation:

> *"There is therefore now no condemnation to them which are in Christ Jesus, who walk not after the flesh, but after the Spirit."* (Romans 8:1)

As we're walking this walk for Jesus, we must constantly remember that we have an accuser of the brethren, Satan, going before the Lord day and night to remind us of our past sins. He also whispers lies in our ears, telling us that we're not worthy to be a witness for Christ. Ironically, there may be times when we believe Satan even though we already know that he's a liar. Once we bite the bait, we begin to wallow in self-pity and hopelessness. This can cause us to throw up our hands with this "witnessing stuff" saying, I've done too many things; I'm not perfect! Well, I have some great news for you! The Bible declares in Proverbs 24:16a the following: *"For a just man falleth seven times, and riseth up again..."* How does a just man or woman rise up again? It's simple. Sincerely repent of your sins and accept forgiveness through Christ Jesus. This allows us to walk in Christ, where there's no condemnation.

Too often, God has forgiven us, but we don't always accept his forgiveness because we haven't forgiven ourselves. Yesterday's gone, and there's no need to beat oureslves up over past sins. Now, does this give us license to willfully sin and throw insincere words of repentance to the Lord? No. Instead, it means that we can rejoice that God has given us a new start and another opportunity to witness of his mercy, kindness, patience and forgiveness.

Moreover, we don't compel people to come to Christ because we're perfect; instead, we do it because God is perfect! The fact that we're not perfect should cause us to have appreciation and gratitude towards him because the Lord still desires to have a relationship with us in spite of our ways. Let's consider the woman at the well again.

> John 4:6-29 *"...The woman then left her waterpot, and went her way into the city, and saith to the men, Come, see a man, which told me all things that I ever did; is not this the Christ?"*

This woman was certainly not perfect, as Jesus called her out for having a colorful history with men; nevertheless, that no longer mattered. Her final conclusion was to tell everyone about her personal encounter with Jesus. It was worth leaving what she was doing in order to proclaim to everyone about the Messiah.

> ***"And many of the Samaritans of that city believed on him for the saying of the woman, which testified, He told me all that ever I did".***

Let's take note of the quantity. Though we do not have an exact number, we do know that there weren't one or two who believed but "many." What if she was stuck in her past sins, and continued to condemn herself over them? It's obvious! Many of them would not have been touched by her testimony and believed on Jesus Christ.

6. Indifference:

"Therefore to him that knoweth to do good, and doeth it not, to him it is sin" (James 4:17).

Did you know that there is a sin of doing nothing, especially when we look at evangelism? Idleness with the things of God tells Him that ***"my agenda, wants and preferences are more important than yours, Lord!"*** Many of us would dare not say this with our mouths, but what are our actions blatantly speaking?

7. Complacency:

Furthermore, idleness goes hand in hand with complacency. Take a look at its definition. Complacency is a feeling of satisfaction with oneself or one's achievements. With the will and work of God, this is absolutely dangerous. A perfect example of such is the one-talented man in the parable of the talents.

> ***"Then he which had received the one talent came and said, Lord, I knew thee that thou art an hard man, reaping where thou hast not sown, and gathering where thou hast not strawed: And I was afraid, and went and hid thy talent in the earth: lo, there thou hast that is thine"*** (Matthew 25:24-24).

This man, like many Christians, received his talent according to his ability with the understanding that he was to **occupy or multiply until the Master returned**. Likewise, God calls us to multiply for Him as well. Why? God is the God of multiplication? God says it numerous times in the book of Genesis (See Genesis 1:22, 28, 8:17, 9:1,7, 35:11).
Multiplication wasn't reserved for the Old Testament alone. Look at the book of Acts.

Acts 5:14 ***"And believers were the more added to the Lord, multitudes both of men and women."***
Acts 12:24 ***"But the word of God grew and multiplied."***
Acts 19:20 ***"So mightily grew the word of God and prevailed."***

Well, that looks like multiplication to me! If we are satisfied with having talents only, we won't strive to multiply because we are already content the way that we are. When I compare myself to myself instead of to the works of Christ, I'll be content with coasting as a Christian without the actively pursuing souls. Moreover, mediocrity will be the standard. In other words, going to church, singing the songs and going through the motions of Christianity is sufficient.

Some people use the excuse that I just live a life before others, and they should know by default. While living a life is important, it is of greater importance to verbally express to others the hope we have in Christ Jesus.

> *"But sanctify the Lord God in your hearts: and be ready always to give an answer to every man that asketh you a reason of the hope that is in you with meekness and fear"* (1 Peter 3:15).

How can we answer someone in silence? Therefore, let us endeavor to multiply until Christ returns.

8. Procrastination:

There are three things that come to mind when I think of this subject. Though this isn't an all-inclusive list, you may be able to bear a witness with one or more of the following items.

I still have time. This statement and way of thinking is furthest from the truth. Moreover, it's one of the leading lies of Satan. If the enemy can convince us that we have all the time in the world, why should there be any rush. This is a common tactic from Satan to cause us to lose our burden and sense of urgency for souls being saved.

2 Timothy 4:2-5 declare this: *"Preach the word; be instant in season, out of season; reprove, rebuke, exhort with all longsuffering and doctrine. For the time will come when they will not endure sound doctrine; but after their own lusts shall they heap to themselves teachers, having itching ears; And they shall turn away their ears from the truth, and shall be turned unto fables. But watch thou in all things, endure afflictions, do the work of an evangelist, make full proof of thy ministry."*

It's pretty clear that the word "instant" requires immediate action. *"In season"* and *"out of season"* implies that there's no off-season for us when it comes to evangelism. We're already seeing people "turning away there ears from the truth" everywhere we go. Let's make full proof of our ministry of reconciliation. Time really is running out.

I've been meaning to do it, but I just haven't gotten around to it yet. There may be many of us who realize the importance of evangelism and sincerely want to witness. Yet, the cares, affairs, and demands of this world keep us busy. Most importantly, they keep us distracted and unfocused on our true mission and purpose in life.

"But seek ye first the kingdom of God, and his righteousness; and all these things shall be added unto you" (Matthew 6:33).

9. Priorities

When I was in graduate school, I was truly overwhelmed. I was working full time as an educator, going to school full-time to meet state-mandated requirements for certifications, and working part time on campus a few days a week to offset tuition. There were church responsibilities, deadlines here, group projects there, and traffic - lots of traffic. I had been lagging behind in my personal evangelism. Any spare time I had was for personal devotion, preparing for work, studying for classes, and sleep. God understood, I thought.

One day I had stopped at a convenience store, which is near my university. This store was located on a busy highway. When I was waiting in line to pay for my item, a rugged-looking gentleman walked up to me, and handed me a gospel tract. He hadn't given one to anyone else. I thanked him and said, "These are the kind of tracts that we give out at my church." He looked at me and nodded but said nothing. As I noticed him heading towards the door, I quickly thumbed through it and looked on the back of the tract for the church address. When I saw that there was no address, I immediately ran after him to ask where he fellowships. After I opened the door, he was nowhere in sight. That's strange, I thought. There was no way he could've gotten into a car and sped off into the sunset that quickly.

I panned the front of the building, and there were only 4 cars in front of the store. One was mine, two of them were parked and vacant, and the last car belonged to a guy who just pulled up and gotten out of his car. Puzzled, I asked the guy if he'd seen the rugged-looking gentleman; "what gentleman?" he replied. Then, I described him to a tee. He shrugged and shook his head saying, "there was no one here... no one came out of the building when I pulled up." I ran back into the store to ask the cashier if he'd seen a rugged-gentleman in the store. "I didn't see anyone like that in here today Ma'am!" he said. My heart sank. I walked back to my car and stood there with eyes widened and mouth open.

Could that have been and angel? Possibly. It was crystal clear to me that he was sent as a reminder of what I should have been doing, witnessing! Though I had a demanding schedule, my priorities were out of whack. Does this sound similar to your life? Let's put God's things first. God promises that we'll reap the benefits.

I simply don't want to do it. Usually, when we don't want to do something, we often come up with excuses not to. In Luke chapter 14, Jesus spoke of the parable of the man who prepared a great feast. When invited guest were told that all things were now ready, did they all come running? No.

The Bible says this:
"And they all with one consent began to make excuse" (Luke 14:18).

When examining the excuses that the men made, they were all illegitimate. Let that be a reminder that when we make excuses regarding why we don't do the things of God and evangelize, we're not fooling anyone but ourselves. People, including Jesus, can usually see right through them. Also, Christ died for every excuse we could possibly make. Therefore, let's go before God and ask him to make our desires in line with His. (We'll discuss this more shortly.)

10. Impatience:
"To every thing there is a season, and a time to every purpose under the heaven:
... a time to plant, and a time to pluck up that which is planted" (Ecclesiastes 3:1-2).
Impatience can breed discouragement when it comes to witnessing. Perhaps, we may have visions of 5 million people falling to their knees in deep contrition and repentance unto salvation at the sound of our voices. Then, we may be witnessing, and it seems like no one is responding. Why should we continue this stuff, anyway? Dear Friend: Don't give up! Evangelizing is gratifying. However, we must understand that the gratification may be instant, and it may not be so instant at other times; it's still gratification, nonetheless. We must remember that we cannot put a timetable on our evangelical efforts.

For many of us who have never lived in an agrarian society, we have no concept whatsoever of seed time and harvest. Before the farmer can plant seeds. The soil has to be overturned. This process is painstaking, long, and arduous. It involves taking out rocks, glass, or any other things that would inhibit the growth of the seed. Moreover, the ground has to be overturned repetitively because the topsoil is hardened and dried due to the elements. Likewise, the hearts of the multitudes are hardened and blinded by the prince of this world, Satan.

It's going to take hard, repetitive work for hearts to become softened and the seed of the Word to be planted therein. In spite of this, don't be dismayed. There's something going on behind the scenes in the spirit realm that will manifest as long as we continue. Also, it is hard work to plant the seed and water it, as Holy Spirit would lead us. Regardless, God admonishes us this way: *"And let us not be weary in well doing: for in due season we shall reap, if we faint not"* (Galatians 6:9).

We may not see the results with some people until years later, but stay the course. If we do not allow impatience and discouragement to settle in our hearts, we will finally be able to *"pluck up that which is planted."* This will only happen if we persevere in our witnessing. Such a task calls for being relentless, come what may!

James 5:19-20 *"Brethren, if any of you do err from the truth, and one convert him; let him know that he which converteth the sinner from the error of his way shall save a soul from death, and shall hide a multitude of sins."*

This is the ultimate goal, building the kingdom one converted soul at a time.

11. Lack of Prayer:
"The effectual fervent prayer of a righteous man availeth much" (James 5:16b).

Though this is the last item mentioned on this list, it's certainly not the least. Prayer has been mentioned quite often in this book, but the importance of it can't be stressed enough! When we pray aright, all the other items on this list will be dispelled!

Even as a celebration takes place in heaven when a soul give his/her life to Christ. The Lord gave this song to our senior pastor while prayer walking in Hawaii and we sing it at our church once someone has gotten saved. The words are as follows:

> *There'll be one more added to the kingdom, praise the Lord*
>
> *There'll be one more added to the Kingdom, praise the Lord*
>
> *When we witness and we pray*
>
> *Letting the Lord have His way*
>
> *There'll be one more added to the kingdom, praise the Lord*

Prayer fuels Evangelism! When we become prayer-less, we thereby become fruitless. With prayer and intercession, the dead souls must arise and come forth even as Jesus commanded Lazarus. As a result, all who have received the Great Commission also received the obligation to intercede for all saints to dispense rivers of living waters. There's no such thing as too much prayer.

Prayer Should Change Us First
> *"Who shall ascend into the hill of the Lord? or who shall stand in his holy place? He that hath clean hands, and a pure heart; who hath not lifted up his soul unto vanity, nor sworn deceitfully"* (Psalms 24:3-4).

Prayer changes the person who prays first. If my hands aren't clean, my mind isn't clean, my mouth isn't clean, or my relationships aren't clean; it would be downright foolish of me to think that God should hear me. I can't draw near to God without acknowledging and repenting of any un-confessed sin. When asked the secret of his spiritual power, Charles Spurgeon said: *"Knee work! Knee work!"*

Nehemiah was such a man whose prayer-life not only changed him, but also started a revival. He confessed his own sins and the sins of the people. During every phase of rebuilding the wall, he prayed unto the Father. Such consistent communication with the Lord led to spiritual discernment, unity while repairing the breaches in the wall, and boldness to stand up against the enemy. He never forsook the opportunity to pray about everything. As a result, one man's prayers ignited a spiritual and social reform throughout all Jerusalem. You might be saying: **We're under grace, and we need a New Testament example.** Well, let's consider the Book of Acts.

An example of such powerful prayer can be found in Acts 1 & 2. They were all in unity and one accord as they prayed corporately, awaiting the *"promise of the Father"* (Acts 1:4-5, 8). The fervent effectual prayers of this 120 people not only ushered in the Holy Spirit until all were filled, they were all changed speaking with diverse tongues *"the wonderful works of God"* (Acts 1:14-15, 2:1-11). Moreover, fearful Peter became as bold as a lion, preaching repentance and remission of sins through Jesus Christ under the unction of the Holy Spirit (see Acts 2: 14-40). As mentioned earlier, the outcome was an astonishing 3,000 souls being saved and added to the church. What a revival! In fact Peter, and the Apostles set the template for being filled with the Holy Ghost and preaching the Word of God boldly.

If you need an even more modern example, ponder this: While in prayer the Lord showed my pastor that **a pastor who had been pastoring for over 40 years was not saved.** Being lead of the Spirit, gird with love and wisdom my pastor went to share what God had shown him. The pastor (*though not exactly thrilled with what he was hearing*) asked what he must do to be saved. At that instant, he received Christ.

This is the result of fervent prayer.
Prayer in the upper room led to Peter preaching to the multitudes (see Acts 1:14, 2:1-4, 2:14-41).
After Peter and John were threatened for healing the lame man, **they prayed and were filled with the Holy Ghost** (see Acts 4:29-33).
Peter was **praying on the housetop** before he preached his first message to the Gentiles, and the Holy Ghost fell upon them (see Acts 10:9-10, 34-48).

Prayer Aligns Our Will to God's
*"**Delight thyself also in the Lord: and he shall give thee the desires of thine heart**"* (Psalms 37:4).

According to Strong's Concordance, the word *"desires"* in its original context and translation here is rendered as the following: request, desire, petition; from the root prayer.
The more we pray fervently, the more we die to the flesh. The more we die to the flesh, the more in-tuned or connected we become with our Father, as mentioned previously. As we become more connected with the Father, we begin to know the will, mind and heart of the Father. The more we abide in Him, we begin to take on more of His attributes, and side with His position on every facet of life. What pleases God therefore pleases us. What grieves the heart of God will grieve us also. As a result, His desires become our desires when we delight or take pleasure in Him. In fact, ***our Heavenly Father desires that none would perish, "but that all should come to repentance"*** (2 Peter 3:9).

It is no wonder why Jesus Christ, Himself, is called **"The Desire of All nations"** in Haggai 2:7. All people groups, which cover the face of the planet, do not know this. Therefore, they worship false deities. The goal is to pray that all will come to know and serve the true and living God.

If our desire is to win souls, He will give us the desires of our hearts because He desires this for us. If we look back over our lives to see all the things we've desired badly enough (legally), we usually went after them, right? Moreover, we probably counted the cost, were willing to sacrifice, and go to great lengths just to obtain those things. It should be no different with soul-winning.

Jesus was the ultimate example of this at the Garden of Gethsemane. Our flesh and carnal mindedness is an enemy of God (see Romans 8:7). **We must wrestle in prayer to put our bodies under subjection.** This doesn't suggest a masochistic notion but rather discipline in persistent, prevailing prayer in order to be aligned with the Father. He went beyond Himself in prayer saying, **"nevertheless not my will, but thine, be done"** (Luke 22:42). May that also be our silent cry with every breath.

Prayer Stirs up a Burden for Souls

"Therefore hell hath enlarged herself, and opened her mouth without measure: and their glory, and their multitude, and their pomp, and he that rejoiceth, shall descend into it" (Isaiah 5:14).
Let's visualize that for a minute. Can you see it? Those who smile at you every day including relatives, neighbors, friends, coworkers and passersby's pouring into hell by the droves should startle us. C.H. Spurgeon once said, "Winners of souls must first be weepers of souls." When is the last time you prayed for souls to be converted? Better yet, when is the last time you wept over the condition of souls and their fate? We've all been guilty to some extent of such lack of prayer.

At first, praying for the lost might seem like picking up weights after a 5-year lapse of not working out. Yet, don't be dismayed! As you continue, something interesting and miraculous will begin to happen. When you begin to think on the state of your own wretchedness and depravity before Christ and hindrances to salvation; then, your prayers for others will become more passionate and ardent as you consider their spiritual state. Continue in such prayer until God releases you. Keep going, and you will develop a burden for souls.

"And shall not God avenge his own elect, which cry day and night unto him, though he bear long with them? I tell you that he will avenge them speedily. Nevertheless when the Son of man cometh, shall he find faith on the earth" (Luke 18:7-8)?

God will answer when we diligently seek him for souls. Why, there's so much to pray for, it's baffling that we can ever come out of prayer. This doesn't negate the many responsibilities that we all have; rather, it's the attitude of prayer and interceding for souls while, cooking, driving, mending, working, washing, and etc. Then, when we get in our private closets, we can earnestly pour out pleadings and intercessions for souls that will cause God to put hands on our prayers and perform His will in the earth.

Chapter 5 Review

Hindrances To Witnessing

Chapter Theme

Evangelism is an easy mandate, however Satan will make it seem an impossible assignment. He will fight you tooth and nail using every weapon at his disposal. He will distract you or hinder your attempts to evangelize by imploring fear, doubt, secret sins, self-condemnation, indifference, procrastination, impatience and prayerlessness. In spite of Satan doing his job faithfully, we too are equipped to do our job of evangelism faithfully. The tactics that Satan uses against the saints are explored in this section.
Futhermore, this chapter teaches you how to eradicate the hindrances of Satan, and witness successfully.

Questions For Reflection

1. Has Satan been able to trip you up because you failed to recognize that he is an enemy of the Christian who is seeking to obey the Father and witness of his love?
_____
_____
_____
_____

2. How has your witness been hindered by the faithful and diligent work of Satan?
_____
_____
_____
_____

3. Has the political correctness of our nation been used as a hindrance to keep you quiet, complacent and at ease in Zion?
_____
_____

Exploring God's Principles For Witnessing

1. We have an _____ of the brethren, Satan, going before the Lord day and night to remind us of our past _____.

2. We don't _____ people to come to Christ because we're perfect; instead, we do it because God is perfect.
When we make _____ regarding why we don't do the things of God and evangelize, we're not _____ anyone but ourselves.

3. If we are satisfied with having _____ only, we won't strive to _____ because we are already content the way we are.

4. If you do not allow _____ and _____ to settle in your heart you will reap an abundant harvest of souls.

5. When we become _____, we thereby become fruitless.

6. Consistent communication with the Lord will lead to spiritual _____, _____, and _____ to stand against the enemy.

Applying God's Principle For Witnessing

Thinking It Over
1. Have you found yourself procrastinating with your responsibility to evangelize by believing you have more time, you will get around to it later, and/or that there are more important priorities right now?
_____
_____
_____

2. Have you been hindered because you placed a timetable on your evangelistic efforts?
_____
_____
_____

3. Since all things are not expedient though they may be lawful, is it a light matter that you do or do not press yourself to evangelize?
_____
_____
_____

Praying About It
1. Ask God to forgive you for yielding to the hindering tactics of Satan and return to the mission field.

2. Pray for the eyes of your understanding to be enlightened with truth that there is an enemy who is fighting against your evangelist efforts.

Acting on God's Truth
1. Cast down imaginations of fear, doubt, self-condemnation, impatience, and indifference about your ability to evangelize.

2. Seek ways to plant a Gospel booklet, speak a kind word, help someone or offer prayer this week to someone as you are lead by Holy Spirit.

Return to daily prayer for souls to be converted.

Activity:
During your personal time of devotion this week, please add one or more of these areas to your prayer time. Please feel free to add to this list, as this burden for souls overtakes your heart. May it also fan the flames of revival in us and those around us.
Let us pray for...

Day 1:
The souls of terrorists, persecutors of the gospel in and out of our country, and those hearing the gospel locally and in foreign lands.
The souls of government officials/representatives, judiciary, legislative and the executive branches of our country.

Day 2:
The souls of military (soldiers, sailors, marines, airmen/women police force) and government officials
The souls of educators, school administration, school policy makers, students and school shooters.

Day 3:
The souls of prostitutes, alcoholics, drug addicts, drug traffickers, human traffickers, and victims of human trafficking
The souls of gang members and those incarcerated.

Day 4:
The souls of the backslidden, your sons, daughters, nieces, nephews and other relatives
The souls of your co-workers

Day 5:
The souls of the rich (up & outers), the poor (down & outers)
The souls of the self-righteous who believe they're okay the way they are

Day 6:
The souls in your neighborhood, city/village, and revival in your country

Day 7:
The souls of those in church hearing the gospel to sell out, sell all, and follow Jesus.
Pray for revival in churches. Also pray for church leaders (pastors, prophets, evangelists, teachers, apostles, worship leaders, children's church workers) to preach the uncompromising Word of truth to their congregations by the power of the Holy Spirit.
Pray for Christians to have a lifestyle of evangelism.

Sample Prayer:

Father,
You told us to ask of you, and you will give us the heathen as an inheritance (Psalms 2:8). Today, I lift _____ before you, and I ask for his/her/their salvation. According to your Word, I pray that the eyes of _____ understanding be enlightened (Ephesians 1:18). I pray that _____ heart/s be softened and receptive to the gospel message. Your word says: no man comes to the Father except you draw him (John 6:44). Even now Lord, I lift you up so that _____ will be drawn unto you (John 12:32). You told us in your holy Word that **"Whatsoever [we] shall bind on earth shall be bound in heaven: and whatsoever [we] shall loose on earth shall be loosed in heaven"** *(Matthew 18:18). Lord, with the power and authority that you have given me through Jesus Christ, I bind spiritual wickedness, powers, and principalities that would keep _____ blinded and prevent _____ from receiving Jesus Christ as Lord and Savior (Ephesians 6:12). I loose _____ from the grips of Satan, that he/she/they may turn from a life of sin. I pray that _____ will run to you in repentance as and have a true conversion experience. May _____ see You as that hidden treasure in the field, and sell all to follow you, now and always. Thank You for doing it, Lord!
I pray these things in Jesus' Name, Amen.*

*Feel free to add to this prayer as Holy Spirit would lead you.

CHAPTER 6:

FURTHERING THE GOSPEL

"I will not believe that thou hast tasted of the honey of the gospel if thou canst eat it all thyself. True grace puts an end to all spiritual monopoly."

-Charles H. Spurgeon-

Spreading The Gospel To Other Lands

As stated in Chapter 3, we should support the furtherance of the gospel with our time, prayer, skills, and resources. To that end, we should also finance our local church missions ministries and/or missions organizations that advance the gospel. Some of these include **Voice of the Martyrs** (V.O.M.), **Samaritan's Purse**, **Mission Aviation Fellowship** (M.A.F), and **Africa Inland Mission** (A.I.M). **Chick Publications** has a Missions fund to which you can donate; this publication mails gospel tracts free of charge to foreign lands, which ask for them. There are many more. Every missions endeavor needs support. Whether we can set foot on foreign soil ourselves or simply send relief, we are to act as joints of supply for those who are on the frontlines of missions (Ephesians 4:16).

Be mindful that foreign outreaches are not the only missionary fields. Our neighborhoods, schools, families, work places, and where ever we travel are filled with souls hungry for the Bread of Heaven. From personal experience, I organized a prayer group on campus while in undergraduate school 6 nights a week in my dorm room for 4 years to pray for souls. Whether people showed up or not, I prayed with the understanding that souls are at stake and continued prayer must be made for them. Several of those who participated in the prayer group are saved, Holy Spirit-filled, and serving in ministry till this day.

When I started in the workforce, I organized a small prayer group with a handful of co-workers that started before or immediately after work. God moved in such awesome ways that a number of individuals received Christ and some began to attend a local church in their quest to become a disciple. Can you organize a prayer group where you are? Let Holy Spirit lead you regarding when, where, and how often to meet?

Whatever you think of doing, ask God for creativity because there are many restrictions and laws that prohibit evangelism in schools and in the workplace. In the United States, students have more freedom to promote and spread the gospel than staff members. Regardless, be sure to ask God for wisdom with spreading the gospel in school or at your workplace. In addition, we should be major assets in our workplaces. In other words, our performances should testify of the excellent God that we serve. If you're a slacker, you make Christ look bad. Most importantly, people won't really take you seriously for Christ.

Gospel Tracts
When furthering the gospel, we should make a concerted effort to invest in purchasing gospel tracts from our local Christian bookstores or online. Gospel tracts are mini booklets that preach the salvation message. When purchasing them, please ensure that the tract has sound doctrine. Tracts from the Fellowship Tract League, **Tractplanet.com**,

Chick Tracts at **Chick Publications,** and Ray Comfort's **store.livingwaters.com** are some to consider just to name a few.

The purpose of the tract is to accomplish the following:
Serve as an icebreaker: It could be considered a conversation starter. You could say, "Good (Morning, Afternoon, or Evening!) May I please give you a gospel tract?

2. Serve as a tangible way to spread the gospel if you only have limited time with person. If you're in passing and have a few minutes to point someone to Jesus, a tract is the ideal tool.

3. Serve as a means to follow up with someone. If you see a person on a consistent basis, you could ask if the person read the tract you gave him/her. If he/she responds by saying yes, you could then say, "What did you think of it? Did you agree or disagree?" If the person hasn't read it, tell them **"You're missing out! That's a really good one your passing up...it's a must read!"**

Sometimes, we might make evangelism more complicated than what it really is. Evangelizing can be as simple as giving a gospel tract in the following ways:

*An attendant at a local gas station
*Auto mechanic or any repair shop
*An attendant at a tollbooth
*A parking attendant
*A Taxi/Uber/Lyft driver
*A bus driver
*Someone sitting next to you on the bus or train
*Car wash attendant/s. Make sure you leave a nice tip to bless them!
*Placing gospel tracts in envelop/s when paying your bills. (If you don't have auto-pay, it is important to pay bills on time in order to maintain the proper testimony and send the right message to the bill collector.)
*A cashier after check-out is completed
*A bank teller at the counter after a transaction, or at a drive-thru
*A server at a drive-thru restaurant.
*Hand a generous tip in a Gospel tract to a server while dining-in at a restaurant. (Please note: we are not to mistreat the people who are serving our food, only to send a conflicting message when giving them a Gospel tract. If we treat people as if we are superior to them, they will feel and know it!)

I personally love to interact with airline pilots and flight attendants. Most of us can relate to boarding a plane, stowing our carry-ons, sitting down and watching other passengers do likewise. Therefore, I deliberately pick out my favorite Christian T-shirt or hoodie with a strong Gospel message because people are forced to read my attire while I'm walking down a narrow aisle to find my seat. Pilots, flight attendants, and passengers alike have complimented me on my gear! It has also sparked some great conversations about Christ. I once gave a Gospel tract to a flight attendant; she looked surprised and said, **"I keep getting these from passengers... I think I better read this one!"** I told her that God's definitely been trying to get her attention; then, I encouraged her to read it on her break, especially the last page where the Sinner's Prayer can be found.

When the doors shut and your flight takes off, no one can run from you then! The person sitting next to you could be a captive audience. Why not give him/her a tract? I usually smile and introduce myself to the person sitting next to me on the plane in order to break the ice. Afterwards, I may ask where he or she is headed, then tell my travel plans. I am deliberate in mentioning "Jesus" or "church" while conversing. When small talk is almost done, I pull out my bag of snacks and ask if she/he would be interested in sharing my food. It usually smells so good, that s/he can't resist. Whether these passengers have declined or accepted, my goal is be extremely courteous and let them know why: Jesus!

There was once a gentleman, who was seated next to me on a flight. I proceeded to begin with the small talk. As we conversed, he mentioned how he and his family used to go to church, but things had changed. It had become very obvious to me that he had fallen away from the Lord. Immediately, Holy Spirit led me to give him a tract. He began reading it; shortly thereafter, he became fidgety as his face turned red. I could tell that he was under deep conviction of the Holy Spirit. After he had finished reading the entire tract, he turned to me with tears welling in his eyes saying, **"Thank you for this! I used to be very active in the church and with the things of God, now I know what I have to do!"** I left him alone for the duration of the flight and let God deal with his heart! As we were about to land, he gave me 2 meal vouchers saying, "my wife works for this airline...these are for you!" I declined, but he insisted that I take them because he was so overcome with gratitude. Look at God! We were both blessed by the encounter! Hallelujah for that!!!

If a person seems totally disinterested in having a conversation, don't push it. I usually wait until we're about to land to hand him/her a tract, saying: "it was nice to meet you! If you're ever in this area (of the address found on the back of the tract), feel free to stop by!" They usually take the tract and thank me; then, we go our separate ways. Sure, I've had a young man pull his blanket over his head to go to sleep in order to avoid a conversation with me. However, there was no offense taken; at that point I remembered that I'm only a messenger. I'll take my delivery elsewhere!

Also, if you run out of tracts, YOU be the tract! Pray that God would give you a "door of utterance" regarding whomever you will encounter that day (see Colossians 4:3).

In addition, ask Holy Spirit for boldness and wisdom concerning who to approach and how. Then, let the Lord lead you from there.

Group Evangelism
"And the lord said unto the servant, Go out into the highways and hedges, and compel them to come in, that my house may be filled" (Luke 14:23).
Consider joining your church outreach ministry. If you don't have one at your local church, seek the Lord and talk to your pastor about starting one. Wouldn't you love to see more church growth? Well, go get them! Surrounding areas of our churches are in dyer need of revival. Remember, you're not just inviting them to church; you're inviting them to Christ. **By inviting them to Christ, you are inviting them to heaven.**

Preparation
Pray for a successful time of witnessing, and pray for unity amongst the believers who are gathered together. It's also important to pray against any spirit of division, malice, strife, envy, jealousy and competition. In Christ, our goal is not to compete but complete one another. No one should be trying to out-do another or be filled with pride that "I am the better evangelist than you!" There is no place for that in the Body of Christ and for Kingdom Building!

Pray that the tracts will be magnetic and that people can't help but read them. Furthermore, pray for the areas where you will be doing the outreach and against any spiritual strongholds and hindrances that prevent people from receiving the gospel. Also, pray for the Holy Spirit to fill everyone with boldness, discernment, and wisdom. Why? ***"He that winneth souls is wise"*** (Proverbs 11:30b).

Know your audience. Near my church are many who speak French, Creole, and Spanish. To break the language barrier we've purchased tracts in those languages. What languages are heavily spoken near you? I encourage you to purchase tracts in those languages because the people will feel like you care enough about them in order to reach them in their native tongue. If you're not sure what language they speak, consider purchasing some tracts without words. They can look at the illustrations, and still understand the gospel message. Those kinds of tracts are also good for children, who can't yet read. Make sure that you've read the tracts, which will be passed out. Should you encounter the person/s again, you can follow up by asking if they have any questions about what they've read. You won't be able to properly answer questions if you haven't read them yourself.

Go out two-by-two. This is the format that Jesus gave when sending out the disciples (see Mark 6:8). When one person is talking, the other should be praying. No one should be talking over anyone or competing to get his or her point across.

Ask local businesses if you can place a stack of tracts on their counter for customers. Return in a week to see how many people have taken them, or ask the owner or manager how quickly they went. Believe it or not, this works! We do it all the time at my church during our outreach and evangelism time; you would be amazed at how many relationships are built and conversations are had about Jesus with the owners and workers alike.

Presentation
Thankfully, born again Christians do not have a witnessing "uniform" as do some other religious organizations. The beauty is that we have liberty and Holy Spirit to guide us as it pertains to our appearance. However, we must not use our liberties as an occasion to the flesh (see Galatians 5:13). Our presentation should be neat and clean, not sending mixed signals about the God we serve. This also means that we ought not wear anything too revealing, too tight, or anything that might be distracting for those with whom we're sharing the gospel. The last thing we want to be is a distraction. Why? Keep in mind that Satan wants to keep people in darkness, causing many to look for a distraction and an excuse not to listen to the gospel because they would like to avoid conviction at all costs. Let's not give people a reason. Therefore, as stylish as we may be, the goal is to allow Holy Spirit to lead us in practicing discretion when it comes to our appearance. The Bible says this:

> *"I beseech you therefore, brethren, by the mercies of God, that ye present your bodies a living sacrifice, holy, acceptable unto God, which is your reasonable service"* (Romans 12:1).

Here, "service" is rendered "act of worship." Ask yourself this: will what I'm wearing glorify God today? Let that be our measuring stick when we're asking God for guidance. God gave us all that we need to present ourselves as living sacrifices for Him.

Also, there are times when Holy Spirit would tell me, "don't wear that today; wear this..." Whenever I listened to Holy Spirit, I was a happy camper because I may have run into some dignitaries or old friends. There's nothing like feeling embarrassed and wanting to crawl under a rock because we've worn something that we may feel uncomfortable with due to whom we ran into that day. When we're that embarrassed and self-conscious, we can become caught up in ourselves and not the true mission, souls.

This doesn't mean that we should wear ball gowns and tuxedos when evangelizing, neither does it mean that we should wear paper bags over us or turtlenecks and longs sleeves in the summer. Holy Spirit will guide us for any occasion, be it individual or group evangelism. Sure, different settings call for a different type of attire. In any event, we should be trying to witness in everything that we say and do from gardening to a stroll in the park or working on projects. In other words, whether at work or at play, those watching us shouldn't be confused about who we serve.

Nevertheless, when deliberately going out to evangelize regardless of group or individual evangelism, we want to be a tool in God's hand. It does not matter how much clothing you do or don't have in your wardrobe, God already knows about that! Let's do our best by giving God our best. Your best may not look like someone else's, but that's fine also. Our presentation should have some middle ground, where we can attract all types for Christ.

"I am made all things to all men, that I might by all means save some" (1Corinthians 9:22b).

This does not mean that we become a sinner to the sinner, in order to win the sinner. Rather, it means that the Lord not only orders our steps, but he also should be able to fashion us as he chooses and lead us even against our preferences.

Why? Because *"we have been bought with a price, and our lives are not our own"* (1 Corinthians 6:20). In essence, it's really not about US! It's about "[saving] some." Otherwise, we will be sending a conflicting message about what we preach. Believe it or not, every sinner sizes us up to determine whether they want to listen or not. I praise God for a Christian group from a local church that I have seen over the years at the beach. Though dressed very casually, they are there every Sunday afternoon witnessing and presenting themselves as beacons of light on the boardwalk.

Additionally, presentation isn't just relegated to what we wear. Rather, it also refers to our demeanor. While sharing the gospel, do you look angry? Smile. After all, you are sharing good news. Does that mean that I'm asking you to plaster on a smile and look like a cartoon character? No. The joy of sharing the gospel should be visibly seen on our countenances. Also, some conversations might be funny. Laugh! It's ok, really! However, don't diminish the seriousness of the message of Christ.

Chapter 6 Review

Furthering The Gospel

Chapter Theme

Most of the time we are guilty of saying we don't know how we can be used by God to further the gospel message. We sometimes fail to see that there are people in our sphere of influence, who are ignorant to the Savior's love. This is not just limited to people in developing countries or indigenous people who need Christ.

This chapter will demonstrates the necessity of supporting the preaching of the gospel locally and beyond. Various methods and tools are shared of how to get the gospel to all kinds of people. Examples of how you can personally further the gospel are discussed.

Questions For Reflection

1. Have you missed an opportunity to plant the gospel message because you believed that it is the job of someone more qualified than you?
_____
_____
_____

2. Do you find yourself overwhelmed at the prospect that you might be the only Bible some people will read?
_____
_____
_____

3. Have you been tricked into believing that furthering the gospel is all too expensive, and you do not have any extra money to promote kingdom-building?
_____
_____
_____

Exploring God's Principles For Furthering The Gospel

1. The gospel can be personally supported by my _____, _____, skills and _____.

2. We should make a concerted effort to _____, in purchasing _____ from our local Christian bookstores or online.

3. Gospel tracts serve to be a _____, a tool to spread the gospel when you have _____ time with a person, and as a means to _____ with someone.

4. When we deliberately make a plan to _____ whether individual or in a group we want to be a _____ in God's hand.

5. Foreign outreaches are not the only mission fields, we have our _____, _____, families, _____ and where we travel.

Applying God's Principle For Furthering The Gospel

Thinking It Over
1. How has your understanding of furthering the gospel changed through reading this chapter?
_____
_____
_____

2. Were you ever in the dark or had misunderstandings concerning available resources for evangelism? Do you now see these resources and its use in a new light?
_____
_____
_____

3. Even if you believe yourself to be a shy person, can you now see that you have tools that will speak for you (gospel tracts) so that you can obey the Lord and evangelize?
_____
_____
_____

Praying About It
1. Ask God to forgive you for your lack of investing your time and money into the furtherance of the gospel.

2. Ask God to quicken you through Holy Spirit to recognize doors of opportunity to make Christ known?

3. Seek the Lord for a missions group you can commit to pray for finance so that the gospel will be preached to all corners of the world beginning at home.

Acting on God's Truth
1. What can you immediately incorporate from this chapter in your daily life for outreach ministry?
2. Begin this week by incorporating prayer in your time with God for opportunities to successfully witness of his love.

3. Partner with your church or others in an evangelistic outreach in your neighborhood.
4. Use three methods discussed to hand out gospel tracts this week.
5. Before you leave your home look in a full length mirror and ask Holy Spirit if your presentation is acceptable for the opportunities that will be presented to you today to win a soul.

Chapter 7:

CONSEQUENCES FOR NOT WITNESSING

"Without the black backdrop of our sinful nature and its consequences (God's wrath), the gospel is a big yawn."
-William Farley-

Consequences For Not Witnessing

Contrary to what many people think there are consequences for not witnessing. Let's examine three main consequences for not witnessing.

1. It's obvious! Souls won't be saved.
"The harvest is past, the summer is ended, and we are not saved" (Jeremiah 8:20).

We not only miss out on being co-laborers with Christ, but we also forfeit experiencing the joy of others coming to the saving knowledge of Jesus Christ. Jesus said, ***"I am come that they might have life, and that they might have it more abundantly"*** (John 10:10b). Part of that "more" abundant life is sharing and ensuring that others have it as well. What's the worse that could happen? Salvation?
"Lost people matter to God, and so they must matter to us." Keith Wright

2. We will contribute to a generation of Godlessness.

"One generation shall praise thy works to another, and shall declare thy mighty acts. I will speak of the glorious honour of thy majesty, and of thy wondrous works" (Psalms 145:4-5).
It's quite evident that someone dropped the ball on this one. Could it be any of us? We live in a generation with full-grown adults who've never stepped one foot in church in their entire lives. I have met many people who know absolutely nothing about God's word. Sadly, some of them don't even know that the verses are called scriptures. We should not wonder why we see so much mayhem on the news and about us, when there is a culture of people who have no frame of reference concerning what is morally right, other than what the world teaches. This is both depressing and frightening.

Ungodly agendas are being pushed in our schools, governments, and churches. If you and I neglect to "speak of the glorious honour of [God's] majesty and of [His] wondrous works" on the cross of Calvary, who will? Are we waiting for someone else to do it? I don't mean to sound cliché, but we truly are part of the problem if we're not part of the solution. Yes, we are in the last days; however, ungodliness will increase if we are negligent to do our part.

3. *We will reap the penalties of disobeying God's Word!*

   "When I say unto the wicked, Thou shalt surely die; and thou givest him not warning, nor speakest to warn the wicked from his wicked way, to save his life; the same wicked man shall die in his iniquity; but his blood will I require at thine hand" (Ezekiel 3:18).

That's right! We will be held accountable for all the times we should have shared the gospel and didn't. Moreover, we will have the blood of all those we could have reached for Christ, on our hands. When we were to warn people of the wrath to come, we may have been afraid of their reactions or moved by their faces. We may have been worried about losing promotions, friendships, and other relationships by telling the truth. I'll submit, that it is better to have people be upset with you for a season and go to heaven, than to be happy with you now and miss heaven.

> *If ye be willing and obedient, ye shall eat the good of the land: But if ye refuse and rebel, ye shall be devoured with the sword: for the mouth of the Lord hath spoken it" (Isaiah 1:19-20).*

Chapter 7 Review

Consequences For Not Witnessing

Chapter Theme

We often do not see that omitting God's command to evangelize has consequences. The consequences of such sin are just as detrimental to those of adultery; lying and stealing just to name a few. We are equally held accountable for sharing or not sharing the gospel. When we omit evangelizing, we aid the sinner to remain in his/her sin. We are then guilty and will have blood on our hands as they stand in judgment before God Almighty, if they die in their sin.

This chapter discusses three consequences of not witnessing.

Questions For Reflection

1. Will I be guilty if I don't share the Good News with those I interact with daily and they find themselves in hell?

___
___
___

2. God so loved mankind that he gave Jesus. Do I have to give the same love to others that was given to me in order to rescue souls from sin?

___
___
___

3. Is it Christian like for me to rest in my salvation but hope others will find Christ without any input from me?

___
___

Exploring God's Principles For Not Witnessing

1. Three consequences of not witnessing souls. They will not be _____, we will contribute to a _____ generation, and we will be _____ for disobeying the Word of God.

2. Ungodliness will _____, if we are _____ to evangelize?

3. Having a more abundant life is _____ and _____ that others have it as well.

Applying God's Principle For Not Witnessing

Thinking It Over
1. My salvation cost Jesus his life. Must it cost me something if I don't evangelize?
_____
_____
_____

2. How has your perspective of the consequences of not evangelizing changed since reading this chapter?
_____
_____
_____

3. What tools and methods have you been using to effectively evangelize?
_____
_____
_____

Praying About It
1. Pray for an obedient Spirit to warn the wicked of their sin.

2. Ask God to forgive you for being more concerned about friendships, losing a promotion or relationship by sharing the truth of the gospel.

Acting on God's Truth
1. Make a commitment to daily herald the good news everywhere you go and to everyone you meet as opportunity presents itself.

2. Memorize Ezekiel 3:18 as a means to remember the consequences of failing to evangelize.

Chapter 8
BENEFITS OF WITNESSING

"There is no joy in the world like the joy of bringing one soul to Christ."
-William Barclay-

"With Christ, it is impossible to be a blessing without being blessed"
-Bishop Calvin L. Bethea-

EXPERIENCE THE BENEFITS OF WITNESSING

There are benefits to both the person sharing the gospel and the person hearing the gospel. It is impossible for you to be a blessing to someone and not be blessed your own self. God will not forget your work and labour of love (see Hebrews 6:10).

1. Exposing someone to the gospel message

There have been plenty of times when I witnessed to people, and they were not receptive. Nevertheless, God allowed me to encounter them years later, and they are now Born-Again Christians and/or leaders in their local churches. When sharing the gospel truth, we afford people the opportunity to hear about the saving grace of the Lord Jesus Christ. The Apostle Paul made it very clear when he said the following:

"I have planted, Apollos watered; but God gave the increase" (1 Cor. 3:6).

As a labourer or co-labourer with Christ, it's important to understand that our roles might vary with every encounter. At times, God may lead us to simply plant the seed of the gospel truth. There are other times when the Lord may lead us to water only. Then, there are other times when God may lead us to do both. This may look different with each encounter. Regardless, it's refreshing to know that God, Himself, will give the increase. What a blessing and a relief! The Lord shoulders the responsibility of adding the increase, and we get to participate in a phenomenon that will change people's lives forever! How awesome is that?

Furthermore, the newly saved will be eternally grateful for your obedience in witnessing to them. Those who may have rejected you at first may come back and thank you later for your honesty and patience when sharing the gospel, while others did not share the message of eternal life. They will always remember you for your faithful witness to Christ. Therefore, stay the course, and wait in prayerful anticipation.

2. The joy of enlarging the Kingdom of God

"I say unto you, that likewise joy shall be in heaven over one sinner that repenteth, more than over ninety and nine just persons, which need no repentance" (Luke 15:7).

Have you ever considered that we cause there to be exceeding joy in heaven when we obey the will of the Father? Often times, we seldom realize the effects our actions have on others, whether good or bad. Others, not to mention the entire heavenly host, rejoice and benefit when we deny ourselves, and lead someone to Christ as the Father gives the increase. Let's cause heaven to rejoice consistently when we obey the Great Commission.

3. The joy of knowing that you've obeyed the Father

Speaking of obedience, we've already discussed how others are blessed by our obedience to the Lord. However, many of us fail to realize that we get blessed by our obedience to God. In John 15:10-11, the Word of God declares this:

> *"If ye keep my commandments, ye shall abide in my love; even as I have kept my Father's commandments, and abide in his love. These things have I spoken unto you, that my joy might remain in you, and that your joy might be full."*

I'm going to go out on a limb, and assume that we all want to experience consistent joy in our lives. If God commands us to *"go", "bear forth much fruit"* as we abide in Him, *"multiply," "occupy till [He] come[s],"* or simply "be [His] witnesses; it is ultimately for the blessing of Christ's joy remaining in us in addition to building the Kingdom. Why does the scripture say, *"might?"* His joy remaining in us solely depends on you and I. In other words, it's our choice regarding the extent to which we allow Christ's joy to remain in us by doing what He says. Moreover, obeying God's commands not only causes His **joy to remain in us**, but it also causes our **joy to be full**. Therefore, if God commands us to evangelize the lost for Him, and obeying God's commands causes us to be blessed with joy that remains and the fullness thereof, why don't we witness more? Imagine how joyous we could be if we witnessed consistently.

Please note:
Happiness is not to be confused with joy. Joy is a supernatural fruit of the Spirit that allows us to endure even the harshest of situations. Happiness, on the other hand, is conditional and temporal.

4. It's a reminder of God's goodness to you.

There are times in a Christian's life when things don't pan out as we've expected, or we're feeling low and despondent. At such times, I charge you to witness anyway. You might be saying, "Margaret, nothing is going right in my life at this point; why or how could I?" Just do it!

I recall a time in my life when I was experiencing hopelessness because of a series of situations in my life all at once. Very few knew it; I mastered plastering on smiles, but I was torn on the inside. During that time, we were on our annual church trip to Hawaii. One day we had traveled to the beach, to see God's glory and watch the sunset. Because the sand was so rocky, we packed up and went to another beach down the road after being there for almost a half hour.

After arriving at our final destination, my first inclination was to sit on the sand and relax, as did some others in our party. Nonetheless, I felt a prompting to go in the water for a swim. While in the water, I met and befriended a woman from California who said that she noticed me at the other beach where we originally were; she had also left the first beach for the same reason. Though I hadn't noticed her at this beach with hundreds of people, I was quickly reminded that I never know who's watching. I immediately sensed that I had encountered her for a reason.

After some small talk, she began to pour out her heart about why she was in Hawaii and her hatred for her brother-in-law. I told her about the commandment that said, "thou shalt not murder."
As she listened intently to see where I was going with this, I mentioned 1 John 3:15, which declares: *"Whosoever hateth his brother is a murderer: and ye know that no murderer hath eternal life abiding in him."* I explained how she was in jeopardy of not receiving eternal life, and continued to share the truth of the gospel with love. I praise God that her heart was receptive, and she received Jesus Christ as her Lord and Savior as we stood holding hands and praying the Salvation prayer in the water. As I embraced her, she started crying. The next morning, she drove 30 miles across the island to attend the church we were visiting for Sunday morning service.

I shared all this to say that witnessing took my mind off of my situations and me; it helped me focus on the God who is greater than any situation. I believe that while sharing the Word of the glorious gospel, I was thereby quickened by it. The power of the Word began to flow through me, and I began to remember the joy of my salvation; immediately, my joy became full. My troubles seemed to diminish in comparison to God's greatness. What if I would have been caught up in my feelings and circumstances? At that moment, I realized that witnessing serves as a pick-me-up when you're at your lowest point. Try it!

5. God will reward you.
To be more specific, God will reward you whether you have done the will of the Father or not. However, you and I determine what kind of reward we will receive from the Lord by the actions or inactions we've chosen to carry out.

> *"Every man's work shall be made manifest: for the day shall declare it, because it shall be revealed by fire; and the fire shall try every man's work of what sort it is. If any man's work abide which he hath built thereupon, he shall receive a reward"* (1 Corinthians 3:13-14).

Those scriptures get straight to the point. It is of paramount importance that we labor to hear *"well done, thou good and faithful servant"* (Matthew 25:21). What good would it have been if we lived our lives without ever having impacted any for Christ? When our works are tried in the fire, all other things that we deemed more important won't really matter. They will be burned up. When we prioritize and *"seek... first the Kingdom of God and his righteousness, all these [other] things will be added to [us]"* (Matthew 6:33).
Let's get to work, and build the Kingdom of God.

Chapter 8 Review

Benefits of Witnessing

Chapter Theme

Evangelism is not a one-way street of blessing. The benefits for evangelism is not only for the hearer who has been given an opportunity to hear about God's love and provision to spend eternity with him, it is also an opportunity for you to fill your joy in obeying your Savior. In addition, this chapter covers five benefits of witnessing.

Questions For Reflection

1. How has your outlook on witnessing changed, as you are now able to see the benefits?
_____
_____
_____

2. Have you lost the joy of witnessing because you have made it more of a ritual than a delight?
_____
_____
_____

3. Has your own personal situations caused you to lose sight of the urgency to make Christ known?
_____
_____
_____

Exploring God's Principles For The Benefits Of Witnessing

1. As a _____ with Christ, it is important to understand our role with each potential candidate for salvation.

2. Obeying God's _____ not only causes His _____ to remain in us, but it also causes our _____ to be full.

3. Witnessing will take your _____ off your situations and put your thoughts on God.

4. God will _____ you whether you have done the will of the Father or not.

5. Some of the joyful benefits of witnessing are _____ the gospel to someone, _____ the kingdom of God, and _____ the Father's commandment.

Applying God's Principle For The Benefits of Witnessing

Thinking It Over
1. What have you learned about the benefits of witnessing that you never thought of before?
_____
_____
_____

2. Have you been slothful in your effort to witness because you didn't see a clear benefit for yourself or the recipient?
_____
_____
_____

Praying About It
1. Pray for your joy to be restored in delighting to see souls saved.

2. Pray that the benefits of witnessing override your complacency and the cares of this world.

Acting on God's Truth
1. Make a commitment to witness to someone this week when you don't feel like it.

2. Memorize Matthew 25:21 as a reminder of the benefit of witnessing.

Final Words

My prayer is that every person reading this volume would unleash the God-given power afforded to them through Jesus Christ, and be conduits for Him. John 14:12 declares: ***"Verily, verily, I say unto you, He that believeth on me, the works that I do shall he do also; and greater works than these shall he do; because I go unto my Father."*** Therefore, if we "believe on [Him]" and we know that Jesus went unto the Father, the ball is in our court and the responsibility is ours. Many of us have only dreamt of "greater works," but I challenge you today to do those ***"greater works"*** because the world is depending on you. What work could possibly be greater than being a tool in God's hand to save a soul from destruction?

Answer Key
For Exploring God's Principles For Evangelism

Below are the fill-in answers for the questions under the Exploring God's Principle section by chapter. For the questions that may have multiple fill-ins, each answer are separated by a comma to provide the answer for the next portion of question to be filled-in.

Chapter One
1. aggressively pinning a person against a wall, a means to win affection, not for self-glory
2. salvation, persuade
3. honest
4. Holy Spirit

Chapter Two
1. salvation
2. rescued/saved, sins
3. public, spiritual
4. outward, spiritual
5. confessed, believe, repent

Chapter Three
1. God-given mandate, responsibility
2. sacrificial
3. reconciliation
4. saving knowledge

Chapter Four
1. reading, studying, fasting and meditating
2. sin-sickness, discerning
3. schoolmaster
4. vocation
5. spiritually wounded, Jesus

Chapter Five
1. accuser, sins
2. compel
3. excuses, fooling
4. talents, multiply
5. impatient, discouragement
6. fuels, prayer-less
7. discernment, unity, boldness

Chapter Six
1. invest, gospel tracts
2. evangelize, tool
3. ice breaker, limited, follow-up
4. neighborhood, schools, workplaces
5. time, prayer, resources

Chapter Seven
1. increase, negligent
2. sharing, ensuring
3. saved, godless, penalized

Chapter Eight
1. co-laborer, encounter
2. commands, joy, joy
3. mind
4. reward
5. exposing, enlarging, obeying

About the Author

Margaret Adjoga-Otu has been serving as a Evangelist for over 20 years at God's Life Christian Church in Irvington, New Jersey. In addition to working in various ministries in the church, she is over the evangelism and outreach ministry, facilitates women's fellowship, teaches Sunday Bible School, and is also the senior worship leader.

Education is another passion for Evangelist Margaret. She holds a Bachelor's Degree in English /Writing from Bloomfield College, as well as a Master's degree in School Library Media Specialization/ Education Technology from New Jersey City University. She feels very blessed to have served in the capacity as a School Librarian/Educator to children and families for nearly two decades. Born and raised in Newark, New Jersey, she counts it an honor to educate students in same city that she received her early education.

Evangelist Margaret Adjoga-Otu has faithfully ministered the gospel throughout New Jersey, Hawaii and Ghana, Africa with the consistent results of souls being eternally saved. Many souls have been brought to Christ through her burden for the lost, intercessory prayers and the simplicity in which she shares the Good News. Holy Spirit has enabled her to cause hell to become depopulated and heaven to be enlarged. Like the paramedics, she is always showing up on the scene assessing the individual's spiritual condition and ready to administer healing on behalf of the Great Physician (Dr. Jesus).

Contact The Author

Email: biblicalevangelism101@gmail.com

Phone: 929-352-4611

"After a person is saved, I recommend "EXPERIENCE A NEW BEGINNING" by Bishop Calvin L. Bethea as a excellent foundation building and disciple tool".

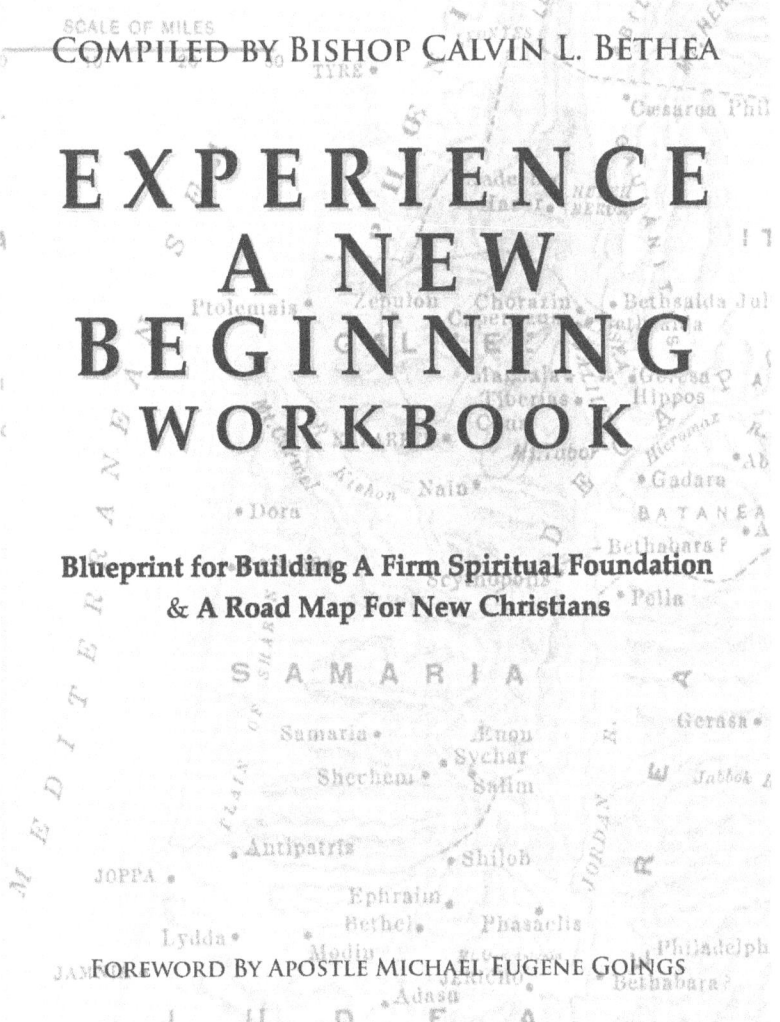

God's Life Publishing is a ministry of God's Life Christian Church, and is dedicated to making resources available to the Body of Christ in the form of printed publications and e-books.

All resources has been reviewed for its spiritual edification content before we publish them for the Body of Christ.

HAWAII
5369 Edgewater Dr.
Ewa Beach, Hawaii 96076
Phone: 973 986-5407

For distributor, dealers, store locations or ordering information:
call or send an email to:
godlife@aol.com

godslifepublishing.org

www.ingramcontent.com/pod-product-compliance
Lightning Source LLC
Chambersburg PA
CBHW081729100526
44591CB00016B/2549